Xmas, 1986

Amel[...]
Bet[...] never!

Ruth & Tex

Knock on Wood

Knock on Wood

BRUCE E. JOHNSON

PHOTOGRAPHS BY
Ray Northway

ILLUSTRATIONS BY
Randy Kraciun

G. P. PUTNAM'S SONS
New York

Designed by Giorgetta Bell McRee

Library of Congress Cataloging in Publication Data

Johnson, Bruce E.
Knock on wood.

Collection of pieces from a syndicated newspaper
column of the same name which began publication in 1979.
1. Furniture—Repairing.   I. Title.
TT199.J6   1984   749'.1'0288   84-4743
ISBN 0-399-12978-2

Printed in the United States of America

*T*o my faithful and vigilant readers
dedicated to preserving a small
but important part of our cultural
and family heritages.

Acknowledgments

I would like to thank the following people without whose assistance and cooperation this book could never have been completed: first, my editors, Bill Thompson and Roger Scholl, whose enthusiasm for the project has been surpassed only by my own; editorial assistant Sara Tittle; copy editor Carol Catt; my close friend and photographer, Ray Northway, and my illustrator, Randy Kraciun, who both saw me at my worst but stuck with me to the end; Lesa Pearson, my editorial assistant, who, despite my best efforts, kept me organized; the staff at Renaissance Computers, who set up my word-processing system and patiently answered all my questions; Don Voots and Vern Northway at Classic Auto Repair and Coachworks for their technical assistance; Nancy Kennedy of Re: Antiques, Allan Weinstein of The Barn and Norma Meyers and Bill Trautman of Country Cousins Antiques for letting us turn their showrooms into photography studios.

And finally, the two most important people, my shop manager, Mike Pitlick, who kept our business going and our clients happy while I pecked away at my word processor, and my wife, Grace, who first encouraged me to start *Knock on Wood* and who has always been able to say the right thing at the right time to keep me going. To all of you, all of my friends and family and, of course, all of my readers, I wish to say "Thanks."

Contents

Introduction

The first "Knock on Wood" newspaper column appeared early in 1979 in the *Collector's Journal,* a small eastern Iowa antique weekly. Less than three years later the column was being read in all fifty states and had been hailed as one of the most reliable sources of practical information on antiques and antique-furniture restoration. Since its beginning, readers have responded with hundreds of letters on nearly everything from buying oak iceboxes to choosing a paint-and-varnish remover to cleaning and polishing brass hardware.

It was only a matter of time, then, until the first collection of columns would be assembled in book form. Categorized under chapter headings, the questions and corresponding answers and tips offer a unique blend of both reader and author firsthand experiences in a format that, hopefully, will be both interesting and informative. Since no two antiques are alike, however, we cannot always assume that the solution to one restoration problem will automatically work for another. I urge you to make it a habit to first test any suggested procedures, materials, or formulas on an inconspicuous spot on your antique. If you sense that you are not witnessing the expected reaction, stop immediately. As much as we would like to, neither I nor the publisher can promise that your antique will respond the same as ours or those of our readers, nor can we assume any legal responsibility for those that do not. Rest assured, however, that unless otherwise specifically stated, all of the solutions, tips, opinions and suggestions in *Knock on Wood* have evolved from my own personal experience.

Before the first question, though, bear with me while I preview what will be a consistent theme running through the book. Obviously none of us is the first to own any of our antiques, nor, hopefully, will we be the last. Were it not for the care and concern of our predecessors, it would not be possible for us to enjoy and use any of our current—or future—antiques.

There is but one way we can repay this debt and that is to guarantee that future generations will have the same privilege. Days of cutting down round oak tables, of painting brass beds and of soaking the veneer off Empire chests are over. Today our objective is threefold: to preserve that which is original, to restore that which is not and to duplicate that which had been.

Then, enjoy.

BRUCE JOHNSON
October, 1983

Knock on Wood

1 / Getting Off on the Right Foot

I s it worth refinishing? Am I going to ruin its antique value if I do refinish it? How do I figure out whether or not it should even *be* refinished? How do I get started?

These and a dozen similar questions face every one of us who decides to tackle a refinishing project. The answers aren't always easy to come by—nor are they always ones we want to hear—but they do give us some guidelines we can use to determine if we are on the right track.

A midwestern reader asks an important question that for too long has kept many refinishers from ever opening a can of paint-and-varnish remover:

Q. Will refinishing lessen the value of my antiques? I read in a magazine that it will and that antiques shouldn't be refinished. I have been refinishing for several years now and am afraid that I have done something terribly wrong.

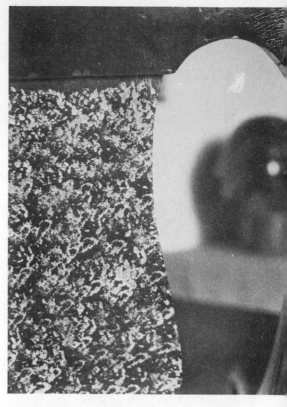

The back of this New England rocking chair was decorated using a technique called "sponging." After a black base coat had dried, a sponge was dipped in white paint and dabbed over the black. Well-preserved examples are highly valued, thus we find another candidate for cleaning rather than stripping.

A. There is a misconception regarding antiques and refinishing that needs to be clarified for everyone—antique collectors, dealers, auctioneers and refinishers alike. Some antiques are definitely more valuable in their original finish, regardless of its condition, than newly refinished. The best examples of this are Early American pieces that were hand stenciled or painted with homemade paints. Many of these were crafted from softwoods, such as pine and poplar, that the craftsmen did not consider attractive enough to be displayed in their natural state. Their early painted finishes were often crude, but are valued and preserved simply because they represent some of the few surviving examples of legitimate handcraftsmanship.

This philosophy, however, does not automatically apply to furniture of later periods, most notably the Victorian, from which so many of our now popular oak, mahogany and walnut antiques come. Furniture from this period was almost always mass-produced with standard factory finishes similar but not superior to our present-day varnishes, lacquers and oils. When these finishes age they crack, peel and darken to the point where the original beauty of the wood is hidden, distorted or even endangered. Proper restoration, whether it be a matter of saving the original finish and adding more protection to it or removing it entirely and applying a new finish, will, in fact, increase the value of these antiques rather than decrease it.

As evidenced by the drawer on the top, which has been stripped, and the one on the bottom, which has not, the late Victorian oak kitchen cupboard to which they belong will be more attractive and more valuable once the dark old finish is removed and a new finish applied. Note how the pressed carvings on the bottom drawer are barely evident under the old finish, which, by the way, would have been clear when it was new.

Note the patina on the arm of this New England rocker dating back to the 1830s. Stripping would destroy it and part of the rocker's value, just as patching the spot where the spindle has worn through the arm would.

Q. What is meant by the term "patina"? Does refinishing destroy it?

A. Although the term patina originally referred to just the tarnishing of metal, it has been adopted by antique-furniture collectors and is tossed about quite loosely by many unaware of either its significance or its relationship to refinishing.

Simply stated, patina is the mellowness that an antique acquires after many years of exposure to sunlight, air, dusting, polishing, crayons and chocolate milk. Not only does the wood acquire a patina, however, but the finish develops its own as well.

Stripping an antique of its finish destroys that part of the patina. That is why it is imperative to clean an antique before stripping it to determine whether or not the original finish can be saved. Refinishing—make that *proper* refinishing—will not destroy the patina of the wood. Improper refinishing, employing harsh strippers, scrapers, coarse sandpaper or excessive sanding, will in a matter of seconds erase what it took a hundred years to create, and will leave you with an antique that, in addition to being almost worthless, looks more like a modern reproduction than a hundred-year-old piece of craftsmanship.

This dough box dating from the Civil War era is constructed from hand-planed, wide pine planks, using square nails. Originally it was painted red, but later had a coat of gray applied. Even so, stripping it down to clear pine would destroy much of its value.

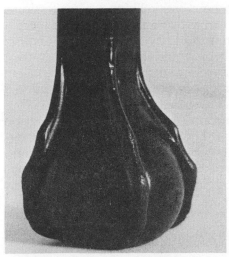

Hand-painted and false-grained pieces aren't the only ones that shouldn't be stripped. This claw-and-ball foot from a Chippendale-style chair made in Philadelphia shows what is meant when we talk about the patina of an original finish. Stripped and refinished it would look more uniform, but would have lost much of its character.

. . .

Once the dilemma of "refinishing vs. value" and the mystique surrounding an antique's patina are clarified, another problem arises, namely:

Q. How do you decide if something is worth refinishing? We have several old pieces of furniture in our attic that were in my parents' home, and I would like to use some of them now in mine, but don't know if they are worth refinishing. I know they would have to be refinished before I could use them, because they are dark. Can you tell me how I can determine if they are worth doing?

A. There are several criteria that should be considered, two of which you have already mentioned: one, you have a use for the pieces and, two, they are family heirlooms.

Deciding whether or not the piece itself justifies the investment of both time and money required for a proper restoration is a little more technical. Generally speaking, though, if it is made of good wood, is structurally sound and doesn't have any obvious major flaws, such as missing veneer, ripped upholstery, warped boards, etc., it probably is worth restoring.

Bring any pieces you are considering refinishing down out of the attic and begin simply by cleaning them with a rag dipped in mineral spirits. You will be surprised how much of the darkness is simply dirt and old wax. Once they are cleaned you can make a better assessment of their condition.

At this point, I would recommend calling in a professional antique appraiser. He or she can tell you how much each piece is worth, both in its present condition and were it restored, and can advise you whether any of them would be worth more in their original finish as opposed to being refinished. In addition, call in a professional refinisher to give you an estimate on how much it would cost to have each piece restored.

You can save yourself a portion of the cost of the restoration by doing the refinishing yourself, but make sure you aren't overestimating your refinishing abilities, especially when irreplaceable family heirlooms are involved. The little bit of savings may pale in comparison to the difference in value between a poorly refinished piece and one that has been done properly.

Another reader addresses the same problem more specifically:

Q. I have a small problem I hope you can solve.

I have a china closet that probably isn't too old. It is walnut (on the back it is so stamped) and has a metal plate that reads "Gimbel Brothers/Philadelphia/New York." The legs are wood claws.

My dilemma is that someone has painted it. I'd like to remove the paint and refinish it myself. I don't think it is worth the expense to have it done professionally—right? However, is it worth all the work I'll go through? Should I just go ahead and repaint it and use it as it is?

A. I think you have several options available to you, but choosing one will have to be your decision based on how much the china closet is worth to you, how much you want to put into it and what it would cost to replace it with something you like as well.

Personally, I wouldn't repaint it without first eliminating all other possibilities—and even then I'd have to really think it over. And over and over and . . .

One possibility, which you mentioned, would be having it completely restored by a professional; another, of course, would

Sometimes it is a good idea to strip just one section of a piece to see what is underneath the paint. Note the top of this child's cupboard. This piece had originally been stained cherry before someone painted it green years later.

be doing it yourself, but regardless of what you decide, I think it would be wise to first have it appraised and an estimate made of the restoration costs.

If you choose not to have someone else restore it, consider paying a professional just to strip off the old paint, since that will be the messiest part of the project. You may want to begin by just having one drawer stripped so you can see what the wood is like underneath. Providing you like what you see, you could have the rest of the piece stripped and then complete the restoration work yourself—a happy compromise any negotiator would be proud of.

Tip—Take color photographs of your projects both before and after restoration. The first can help document original color, design and highlights, especially useful with projects spanning several months. The latter can be invaluable for insurance appraisals in case of fire, theft or vandalism.

. . .

Special problems always seem to pop up—sort of like loose veneer—that can make even an experienced refinisher wonder why he never went into cabinetmaking:

Q. I have an old treadle sewing machine that had been my grandmother's. I haven't done much refinishing, but I was thinking about stripping it and putting on a coat of varnish so I could use it as a plant stand.

The veneer is missing in several places around the lid, and one of the drawers is stuck. Do you think it is worth refinishing, and is it a good project to start with?

A. Old treadle sewing machines present several problems—of all which you had better be aware of before tackling one.

First, unless the works, the base and the wood are in near-perfect condition, the machine probably won't be worth as much as it will take to completely restore it. They were literally produced by the thousands (with many more than anyone ever expected surviving countless 4-H sewing projects) and don't offer many practical uses today other than as sewing machines—and plant stands.

Second, their extremely thin veneer is difficult to work with. It is hard to obtain, thus most refinishers end up using regular

Our Improved High Arm in the New Drop Head Case.

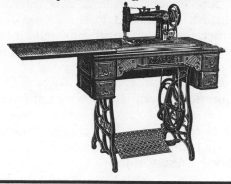

Ad for a treadle sewing machine taken from an 1895 edition of the Montgomery Ward catalogue. The machine could be ordered in two different woods, walnut for $22.00 and oak for $22.50.

---

veneer and sanding it down to the required thickness—or should we say thinness.

If the machine has a good deal of sentimental value to you, the investment in terms of time and money will no doubt seem insignificant. Consider, however, whether or not you want to risk a genuine family heirloom as your initial refinishing project. Perhaps it would be wiser to make those inevitable first mistakes we all end up making on a piece with fewer obstacles to overcome and less personal value.

. . .

Unfortunately, many family heirlooms make their way out of the family, but hopefully most will end up with refinishers as conscientious as this one:

Q. I recently purchased an old child's wagon from a sixty-year-old lady whose uncle had used it when he was a child. The wagon has individual wooden spokes, which are all intact, and metal rims around the wheels. They were originally painted red, but much of the paint has worn off.

The box and floor are wood, unpainted, although there is a band of red trim around the top of the box and it, too, is worn

GETTING OFF ON THE RIGHT FOOT / 23

down to the wood in places. The boards that make up the floor are warped and there are gaps between them.

My question is simple: how should I restore this wagon? Should I just clean and varnish it? Should I repaint the red wheels and trim? The front metal support is broken; should it be welded? What about rust on the axles? And should I replace the boards in the floor?

A. You call that a simple question? I can hardly wait until you have a tough one.

You have brought up several good points that actually apply to more than just your wagon. It brings to mind a slogan used by the National Trust for Historic Preservation:

> *It is better to preserve than repair,*
> *better to repair than restore, better*
> *to restore than reconstruct.*

I would suggest that you first have the broken metal piece welded by someone you can trust to have an appreciation for the antique value of the wagon. What you will want is a neat weld that will not detract from the rest of the piece.

I would then embark upon a good cleaning with mineral spirits for the wood and a rust remover for the metal. I would not repaint, nor would I replace any boards. Keep the wagon as original as possible and it will retain its total value.

Once it is clean and dry you can then preserve it with a coat of varnish if it seems necessary. If you do, don't use a thick, glossy varnish. Instead, thin down a satin varnish with turpentine and brush it on. All you want it to do is protect the wood and keep it from drying out or taking in more moisture.

Tip—Keep a file card on each antique you restore, noting information such as initial cost, repairs made, types of stain used and finish applied. The cards can prove helpful months or years later when you want to match another antique to an earlier one you refinished.

. . .

Probably the greatest overall problem faced by all refinishers when they embark upon a project is capturing the same feeling and appearance a fine antique has in its original finish.

A file card should note how, when and where your antique was acquired, what types of refinishing products were used and other pertinent information. Before and after photographs of your restoration projects will complete your records.

Q. I have done some refinishing, mostly on smaller, less expensive pieces, and have purchased several antiques from dealers who had either refinished them or had them refinished. In both instances, there seems to be a great disparity between the appearance of, for instance, a fine round oak table in its original finish and a similar table that has been refinished. Is there a secret to refinishing antiques in such a way that they don't look obviously refinished?

A. This question has inspired more refinishing books—including this one—than any other single query. I'll try to answer it briefly by touching on what I consider to be the key flaws in many refinished pieces:

Stripping—Old finish left in corners and joints; stripper drips showing on edges, down sides and inside drawers.

Repairs—Wrong type of wood used to patch damaged area; new wood failing to blend in with old.

Sanding—Wood over-sanded, removing all traces of age; cross-grain sanding scratches remaining.

Paste Filler—None used; pores left open.

Stain—Antique stained a different tone than it ever was originally; muddy-looking stain.

Finish—Wrong type of finish applied; runs and sags on sides; drawers left unfinished.

Rubbing Out—None done; dust particles left in finish.

The goal should not be just to change the finish, but to restore a piece so well and so entirely that no one would even guess that the finish wasn't original.

For refinishers, the greatest compliment is no compliment at all.

2 / The Early Bird Catches the Antique

Before we can even begin to think about cleaning, repairing, refinishing or even dusting our antiques, we have to have them. The easiest to come by—but, ironically, the most important— are those that are in the family. Your great-grandfather's porch rocker is more than just another piece of furniture: it represents a portion of your family's history and your great-grandfather's personality. Rocking chairs, like worn kitchen tables, were often the site of great family debates, the place where problems were solved, newspapers read and babies rocked.

Family antiques, unfortunately, are becoming more and more scarce. We are lucky if we have one or two pieces in our household that survived countless moves, changes in styles, breaking up of households and auctions. We cherish them dearly, but know that there just aren't enough to go around. Once the family well has gone dry it's time to find other sources of antiques.

Knowing where to buy antiques is important, but just as important is knowing what to look for, what to avoid and what constitutes a "good deal." Although antique shops and auction houses are becoming more and more professional in their displays and marketing approaches, antiques remain one of the most perplexing items to price. Price guides don't offer a great deal of help, so seller and buyer alike must struggle with the problem of assessing an antique's strengths and weaknesses and arriving at a fair market value for it.

Take for instance, this reader's question:

Q. Recently I listened to two dealers at an antique show talk about how bad business had been lately. They seemed to think prices would be dropping and that, as one put it, the antique boom had "busted."

I've been buying antiques for years, so does this mean some of the things I've bought recently are going to be worth less than I paid for them? I always thought one of the reasons for buying antiques was that they would increase rather than decrease in value. Should we hold off in our buying?

A. Talk to ten different dealers and you'll get ten different opinions on how business has been and what is happening to the price of antiques. Note, though, that I said "price" and not "value."

My observations aren't worth any more than the next person's, but I feel the dealers who have offered good-quality merchandise, kept their prices fair and reasonable and who have offered the little extras, like personal service, help in delivery and free and honest advice, have had a good year and will continue to.

Naturally, the economy has affected the antique business as well as the rest of the business sector, but those who can adjust, survive; those who can't, don't.

As far as prices are concerned, I think we have seen a drop in prices for lower quality antiques and antiques "in the rough," but I attribute that primarily to a drop in demand. Restoration shops report an increase in business, which tells me that people aren't doing as much of their own refinishing as perhaps they did ten years ago.

Top-of-the-line antiques are holding their value and should continue to show steady yearly increases. Regardless of the economy, antiques—especially the good ones—are scarce and are becoming more so each year. And each year there are fewer marble-topped walnut dressers available, for instance, meaning the value of each existing one will go up and not down, regardless of where the prime rate goes.

The bargains are still out there, so don't quit now. If you are a smart buyer, your purchases will be worth more and not less a year after you buy them.

Tip—If you want to buy antiques both to use now and possibly to sell later, buy top quality. Mediocre pieces don't increase in value as fast as good-quality antiques, so if you are looking for a fast gainer, avoid the damaged, chipped or overrepaired pieces. An extra dollar spent on quality will bring you ten when you go to sell.

. . .

Everyone has his or her preference when it comes to shopping for antiques, but we shouldn't forget that every source has its advantages and disadvantages:

Q. My husband and I are in the market for a round oak table and a set of either four or six matching chairs. Our problem is that we disagree on where we should get them. I think we should get them from a regular antique shop, but he says we can get a better deal going to auctions. I don't mind auctions, but don't we take a chance of buying something that might be broken or a fake? Can you take things back at an auction if that happens? That's why I think we should get our table and chairs from an antique shop.

A. We're treading on dangerous ground here, so we'll have to walk carefully.

Both antique shops and auctions have their advantages and disadvantages as far as buying is concerned. Shops offer the convenience of time and attention; you can walk in anytime they are open (though that in itself can be a problem—it seems that many dealers complain that the public does not treat them as professionally as they do other retail merchants, but then most retail merchants keep far more dependable hours than antique dealers) look around, talk with the owner, make a decision and leave.

Auctions, on the other hand, consume a good deal of time waiting for a particular piece to come up for bids; outdoor auctions also put you at the mercy of the elements. With auctions, however, you have the opportunity, we assume, to purchase a table and set of chairs, for instance, for less than their market price. As proof, notice at your next auction who your competition is in the bidding; often it will be antique dealers willing to invest their time, hoping to snap up a good deal.

If you buy through a shop you must expect that part of the price of each antique is going toward overhead expenses, such as rent, restoration and time spent at auctions. Generally speaking, however, dealers stand behind their merchandise and, if for any reason you feel that what you bought was not what you were led to believe you were buying, they will accept returns.

Auction buying gives you the chance to grab a good deal, at perhaps far less than shop price, but it also involves certain risks. For the most part auction pieces are sold "as is," and it is the buyer's responsibility to inspect and, in fact, appraise any antique he or she is interested in. The auctioneer's primary responsibility is to get as much for his client as possible without misrepresenting any piece. If a reproduction is sold as an antique, then a return is in order; however, if you failed to realize that all of the chairs needed regluing, then that is your fault and not the auctioneer's.

My advice to you and your husband would be not to rule out either antique shops or auctions in your search for a table and set of chairs. Both can be a great deal of fun and quite educational. Learn what to look for by talking with dealers, auctioneers and collectors and by comparing antiques seen in different shops with those up for bids at auctions.

Finally, remember that both antique dealers and auctioneers are dependent on their good reputations to stay in business; neither can afford to risk their entire business fortune just to make a single sale. Word will quickly spread about which dealers or auctioneers to avoid; fortunately, word will also quickly spread about which are fair, reasonable and personable.

So how do you recognize who the good ones are? Simple. They're the ones who aren't complaining about how bad business is, because they're the ones the buyers are going to.

Tip—The worse the weather, the smaller the crowd. Bundle up and hit one of the local auctions with your wad of cash. You may come home with the best buy of the year in tow.

• • •

Wise antique buying takes more than just a wad of cash, as this reader is willing to admit:

. . .

Q. I have been looking for months for a set of four pressed-back oak chairs with arms, but had found none until recently when I went to an antique auction held by a dealer who was going out of business. My chairs were there, but in the excitement I didn't take the time to look them over carefully. I guess I was more concerned about how many people were looking at them and who might be bidding against me.

Naturally, I assumed the chairs were mine before the auction even began. As it always happens, several people were interested in them, and I ended up paying more than I now think I should have to get them. They had been refinished and, although they had been stained darker than I would have preferred, from a distance they looked fine. When I got them home and began looking them over, though, I began finding little things that bothered me and I've since become very suspicious. For example, the rungs are all nailed in place and two of the legs aren't exactly like the others. Some of the spindles don't match the others either, and, like I said, the chairs are stained awfully dark. Do you think I made a mistake?

A. That's a difficult question to answer. It does sound like your chairs are far from original, but what you have learned may save you many more dollars in the future.

There are several clues you can look for in spotting an antique that has had extensive and improper repair. First, check out the reputation of the person you are buying from. I would be extremely cautious concerning any pieces being sold at auction by a dealer going out of business, for in the haste of preparing items for the sale someone may have resorted to a "quick and dirty" restoration job.

Second, an unusually dark stain may be hiding a variety of ills ranging from sloppy repairs to a mixture of undesirable woods. Nails tighten loose joints—temporarily. Spindles that are uneven or of various colors may indicate poorly turned replacements; and legs that don't match, well, that's pretty obvious.

Once you have spotted an indication that repair work has been done on an antique, use it as a sign that further inspection is necessary to determine if the restoration work was done properly and if the piece is priced appropriately.

As for your chairs, if you like 'em, use 'em. If not, sell them and keep looking. That's where the fun is anyway.

. . .

While on the subject of auctions, one reader took the opportunity not only to share an experience she had recently but to voice her opinion on what has become a controversial but common practice of auctioneers:

Q. I've got both a question and a complaint. What gives auctioneers the right to sell table leaves separately from the table they belong to? I was at an auction today where there was a square oak table I was interested in buying. I was flabbergasted when the auctioneer announced he was selling the table first and then would sell the leaves "so much apiece, take as many as you want."

I tried to protest, but he just ignored me and started the bidding. The people around me didn't seem to be bothered by it, but I guess they weren't interested in the table either. I was so mad I refused to even bid. A lady I didn't know got the table and then had to buy the five leaves for fifteen dollars each! I thought she was lucky, since someone could have run the price up on her, knowing of course she would want them.

Is this legal? Can it be stopped? I wanted to confront the auctioneer afterwards but the auction ran so late and I was so mad I had to leave. Am I just backward?

A. If you're backward, then don't feel lonely, because I get just as mad as you do when I see the same thing happen. I was at an auction recently when a prominent antique dealer did get the auctioneer's attention and demanded that the leaves be sold along with the table. The auctioneer refused, declaring that the owner had requested they be sold separately.

I agree with you that it should be illegal—and it certainly is already unethical. To me it just shows which auctioneers are concerned more about money than integrity. As for stopping the practice, I'm sure it would take nothing short of the crowd refusing to bid unless the leaves and the table were sold together— which isn't such a bad idea if you can get everyone to hold back.

How about it, auctioneers?

. . .

The previous letter (certainly it couldn't have been my answer) prompted several replies from auctioneers all over the country, most of which were similar to the following:

"It is not because auctioneers are greedy and are out for a fast buck [that they separate leaves from tables]. But if I would be having an auction for the person that wrote in to your column and she had a table like that for sale and I didn't sell them that way, I would not be doing the job I was hired to do. As an auctioneer I am hired to sell that item the best I can and to the highest bidder."

A question then arises: Would this theory—that the auctioneer is duty bound to get the most money he or she possibly can for the client—pave the way for selling a mirror separately from the dresser it was once attached to, a towel bar separately from the commode to which it once belonged or a top separately from the base of a Hoosier cupboard? I'm not accusing any auctioneers of going to this extreme, but my point is that the leaves of a table are as much a part of that table as the mirror is of a dresser. Each of the components listed above can exist on its own and, in fact, would be more useful than a set of leaves without a table.

If this practice ever should become widespread, then we are destined to spend much of our time looking for, or lamenting the loss of, fine, complete antiques. Surely a sense of ethics must enter in somewhere.

And if someone, auctioneer or not, can convince me and our reader that table leaves and the table are two separate pieces of furniture and should be sold that way, please let me know. So far, I'm not convinced.

. . .

Auctioneers and table leaves aren't the only source of problems when buying antiques, as this couple who enjoy attending antique shows will attest to:

Q. We have a big problem and never thought we would run into an antique dealer like this.

Last October at an antique show in Minnesota we found an antique dealer who had a particular cup exactly like what we had been looking for, but she didn't have it with her. She said she would mail it to us when she got home, at least by the first of last month, but she hasn't.

I have written two letters, but with no answers. We paid for the cup with a check, which she cashed right away. I think she has had plenty of time to let us know why we haven't gotten the cup. I don't know what to do. We believe she was really honest, as most antique people respect each other. Could you let us know what to do? The money means something to us and we also really want the cup. We are disappointed to think we can find dealers at shows who are like this.

A. Well, let's not assume the worst yet. Your dealer may still be on the road, or in all the confusion of unpacking after arriving home, may not have had the time to open all her mail, much less adequately pack and send you the cup.

Buying as you did, however, involves a degree of risk. In the future I would recommend a slightly different course, such as paying only an agreed-upon deposit with the remainder due upon receipt of the item in satisfactory condition. Another possibility would be having the dealer send it C.O.D., in which instance you would pay nothing until the item had arrived. There is an extra charge to you for the C.O.D., but it is minimal compared to what you might lose any other way.

(*Note*: Just before press time our reader wrote again, informing us that she had indeed received the cup and a note of apology from the dealer. All's well that ends well.)

Tip—Antique shows have become popular all across the country, with shows scheduled everywhere from river banks to high school gymnasiums to elegant hotels. The best times to attend are either just when the show opens and the merchandise has not yet been picked over or a few hours before closing, when the exhibitors are most willing to be flexible in their pricing.

Tip—Despite—or perhaps because of—minor inconveniences such as 2 feet of snow, icy roads and sub-zero temperatures, January and February are excellent months to go antiquing, at least in the East and Midwest. Dealers are generally short on customers, but are collecting inventory for the upcoming season. Bundle up and go looking for some great deals.

Tip—Don't overlook all those small country antique shops on your treks across the state to yet another antique show. Many times they hold better bargains and a greater opportunity for a surprise find than the heavily worked city shops.

• • •

For those of us living in the right part of the country, yard and garage sales offer the opportunity to buy directly from the

A country antique shop. A short detour off a heavily traveled main road can lead you to a literal gold mine of antiques.

owner—so long as you don't mind sifting through fifteen years' accumulation of kitchen appliances (what else do you do with a worn-out blender or a Vegamatic you only used once?), garden tools and outdated clothes. Once in a while, amidst those green leisure suits, broken hoes and partial Monopoly sets you can find a piece of Heisy glass, a signed Stickley rocker or just a good old library table.

Some of our readers have been generous enough to share with us a few of their tips for successful "yard sale-ing":

Tip—Keep a couple of old blankets and a length of clothesline in the trunk of your car in case you find yourself miles from home and face to face with one of those offers you can't refuse. You may leave looking like the Beverly Hillbillies on their way to Los Angeles, but you'll be smiling all the way home.

· · ·

This reader had the same idea, but with an extra ingredient:

Tip—With yard-sale season in full swing, make sure the trunk of your car is stocked with emergency garage-sale equipment:

some old blankets, a rope and twenty dollars in cash. Like they say, expect the unexpected—then buy it.

Tip—Late fall is an excellent time to get back into the habit of going to Saturday morning yard and garage sales. The number of sales may not compare with those in May and June, but the competition isn't as great—and many times you can stumble into a legitimate garage- and attic-cleaning sale. While everyone else is busy getting ready for football games and the approaching cold season, you could be taking a few hours out to pick up some great late-season bargains.

Tip—Get a jump on the Saturday morning yard- and garage-sale crowd by stopping at those sales that start on Thursday and Friday afternoons on your way home from work.

Tip—I have found that the key to smart shopping is not being a hard bargainer or having a degree in industrial negotiations. It lies in knowing what to look for, in being able to spot a good antique at a fair price amid several questionable ones at just as questionable prices. Regardless of whether it be at an antique shop, an auction or a yard sale, closely inspect any piece you may buy, decide how much you want to give for it and don't waver when the pressure is on.

. . .

And finally,

Tip—The best time to buy an antique is when you see it: he who hesitates, loses out.

. . .

Once you have found where the antiques are—be it at shops, auctions, shows or yard sales—you turn from taxi driver into sleuth. Antiques have become very popular in recent years and thus very valuable, making them an ideal target for forgers. Fortunately dealers and auctioneers can almost always be expected to help screen out imitation antiques, but we shouldn't let ourselves be lulled into thinking that all that glitters is old. A little bit of knowledge and a few minutes of inspection should enable you to spot the obvious forgery and eliminate the apprehension expressed by this particular reader:

Q. I've been interested in antiques for several years now, but I still do not feel comfortable buying what I think (hope?) is an antique but am afraid is a fake. Can you give me any suggestions on what to look for to make sure I don't spend a lot of money on something that isn't worth it?

A. This is a subject books have been written on, for it is a concern of every novice and experienced antique collector. Reproductions in glassware, art, pottery, etc., I won't attempt to discuss, for the subject is far too technical for the amount of space we have here. But there are a few things to look for when buying antique furniture that can apply equally to several different time periods and types.

First of all, you need to be careful, but you don't have to be paranoid. When compared to the number of legitimate pieces, there just isn't that much fake antique furniture out there—and that which is can be spotted without too much trouble. It is only when you get into big-ticket pieces like Chippendale chairs and Belter couches that you need to get into some really heavy research. If you're interested in getting into those types of pieces, then I would recommend buying books on specific styles and bringing in private appraisers for their opinions.

For most furniture we see a quick check for the obvious will suffice: new wood, boards stained on one side but new-looking underneath, new hardware, evidence of planer and jointer marks, and a lack of a true patina are all signs of recent tampering. Most forgers are lazy and won't take the time to counterfeit the parts that don't show, so if you check underneath tops, inside cases and the undersides of drawers, you'll soon spot any questionable pieces.

. . .

Legitimate reproductions (can those two words be used together?) can also pose problems, especially when someone decides to do a very good job of distressing them.

Q. I have been looking for an oak commode to use in my bedroom for some time now and have been able to find several in various woods and conditions. I've been bothered, though, by several that I have seen that looked more like reproductions than legitimate antiques. Is there someone who is making new commodes that look old? Is it legal for antique dealers to sell them as antiques?

A. Reproductions of oak antiques began appearing several years ago as the demand for good-quality antiques began to exceed the supply. The best example of this occurred in California where so many new round oak tables surfaced that it began to depress the price of legitimate antique tables.

There is nothing illegal in an antique dealer selling reproductions in his or her shop just as long as they are clearly identified as such. Laws are broken, however, when a reproduction is misrepresented as being an antique.

It is more likely that the commodes you saw were legitimate antiques that had been "overrefinished." More antique dealers are guilty of overrefinishing—harsh stripping, belt sanding, overstaining, using high-gloss varnishes, etc.—than trying to pass off reproductions as antiques.

And as far as I am concerned, overrefinishing is the worse of the two crimes—at least the reproductions aren't ruined as are the overrefinished antiques. If you find a commode that you like but feel may be a reproduction, check the inside of the case and the drawers for signs of age. Most forgers don't bother distressing the insides and backs of the pieces they are trying to pass off as old. In addition, ask the dealer for a verification on your receipt of the approximate age of the piece. That way if you discover later that it is not what he or she indicated it was, you can demand compensation.

Q. When did furniture makers and builders stop using square nails? Would anything with square nails in it automatically be considered antique?

A. To be perfectly honest, some furniture makers (or fakers) haven't stopped using them yet.

Square nails have been used since our country was first settled and, since they have a way of lasting hundreds of years, still abound. Almost every restoration shop, my own included, has a can of old square nails around to use in repairing antiques that originally had square-nail construction. Naturally, then, if someone were to want to fake an antique, they could find a ready supply of square nails.

Though nails alone can't be used to determine if a piece of furniture is truly an antique, as a general rule square nails were widely used throughout the nineteenth century, but soon after were replaced by a combination of round nails and glued joints without any nails.

Tip—It has been said many times that forgers rely more on the ignorance of their buyers than on their own skills as craftsmen. Use your head before your checkbook.

Q. Can wormholes be interpreted as a reliable indication that a piece of furniture is a genuine antique and not a reproduction?

A. No. Wormholes are caused by termites and certain varieties of beetles, both of which, unfortunately, are alive and well today. Lay a board on a dirt floor for several weeks and you will have proof that wormholes are not reliable indications of age.

Only a few unscrupulous perfectionists take the time and trouble to infest their reproductions with insects to pass them off as genuine antiques. Most resort to more easily detectable methods, mainly using ice picks and small drill bits.

Their fatal flaw, however, comes with their inability to accurately duplicate the erratic tunneling of the beetles and termites. Fake wormholes run straight and true, while genuine tunnels wander about just beneath the surface of the wood. If you feel that a wormhole may be something other than what it appears to be, probe the opening with a thin wire or straight pin. A magnifying glass will help separate perfectly round artificial holes from nature's oblong variety. Obviously, "antiques" with less than genuine wormholes are to be deemed suspect, as are their owners.

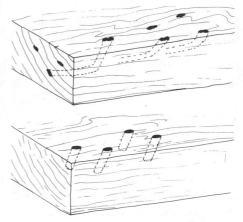

Close inspection can quickly differentiate between real wormholes (top) and the man-made variety (bottom). Unlike a drill bit, powder-post beetles make irregular holes, and their tunnels turn and run with the grain. Either a magnifying glass or a straight pin will flush out a fake.

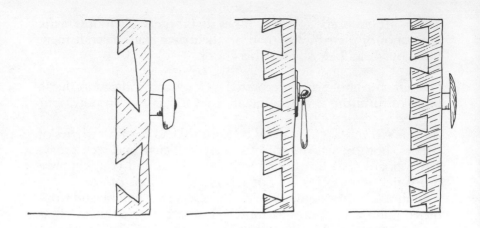

One of the more reliable means of detecting the age of an antique is checking the dovetail joints on drawers. On early pieces the dovetails are generally large, fewer in number and irregular (left); as machines were introduced and improved in the mid-1800s, dovetails grew more regular in spacing, larger in number and smaller in size (center) until by the end of the century they were uniformly sized and spaced (right).

Tip—One of the best ways to determine if a piece of furniture is really old is to look at the dovetail joints at the corners of the drawers. The older the piece the fewer and more irregular the dovetails are, since they were cut by hand. Steam- and electric-powered machinery has enabled factories to cut multiple dovetails evenly since the mid-1800s.

Q. Our family has undertaken as our summer project the restoration of my grandfather's old oak rolltop desk. When we removed the cubbyholes beneath the roll, we found the numbers "2-10" written in chalk on one of the back panels. Could this be interpreted to mean that the desk was made around February of 1910?

A. It is quite possible that the desk was made around the turn of the century, but it is unlikely that the numbers you found were meant to indicate that. Workers in furniture factories mass-pro-

The hand-cut but very precise dovetailing on this walnut lamp table helps place it in the mid-Victorian (circa 1860) era. Note how the craftsman's markings can still be seen between the dovetails. The crack in the side could have been avoided had someone coated the inside with a sealer to keep it from drying out and shrinking.

ducing rolltop desks were less apt to date the pieces they were working on than were earlier craftsmen constructing pieces by hand in their shops.

Numbers such as the ones you discovered often indicated the particular finish, wood or part for a desk and can often be found on the insides of panels, the backs of pieces and the bottoms of drawers.

That is not to say, however, that the numbers couldn't have been intended to date the piece. Other evidence must be taken into consideration, though, before accurately assessing the age of an antique. Compare the style of your desk to those pictured in furniture history books and catalogues. Check for patent dates on the insides of the hardware. Question family members about the history of the piece, but remember, memories are not always accurate.

One of the best means of dating an antique is through the construction techniques and materials used in assembling it. Furniture history books can help identify nails, screws, woods and joints associated with various time periods in cabinetmaking. Through not one but several sources you should be able to accurately date your desk. As with all such marks and labels, though, do not destroy the numbers you have found. Future research may shed a different light on them.

Q. My partner and I are searching for a rolltop desk to use in our business office. We have decided to get an oak, S-curve model and have looked at dozens in the past few months. Before we can settle on one desk, however, we want to lay an argument to rest.

Several of the desks we have seen have a slot cut in either side about an inch below the groove in which the roll runs. The slot is generally 5 to 8 inches long and can be found on both sides of the desk.

Tell us, please, what was the slot used for? We can't seem to find any possible use for it and none of the dealers we have talked to seem to know for sure.

A. The slots you have described served two purposes. They were designed to permit mail to be dropped into the desk after the roll had been locked for the night, but they also served to ventilate closed desks.

A little imaginative speculation might explain the need for a mail or message slot. As you may yet discover, paper items left atop a closed roll have a way of disappearing down behind the back of the roll if not removed before it is opened. It's not unusual for a new owner to find letters, papers and occasionally currency behind the roll of an old desk when it is dismantled either for transportation or restoration.

As for the need for a ventilation slot, lock your lunch in your present desk over the weekend and see if you don't drill ventilation holes Monday morning.

. . .

While coming face to face with a legitimate illegitimate antique is not an everyday occurance (and hopefully will remain that way), there are a few other mental obstacles to be overcome before many people feel confident about antique buying. Here's a good example:

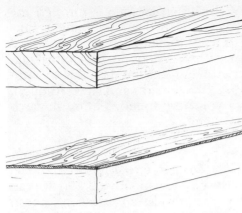

If you look closely at the edge of any board you will be able to spot veneer by following the grain lines. Here the top board is solid, while the bottom one has had a layer of veneer applied.

Q. I bought at an auction this summer a buffet that I liked and wanted to go with my dining room table and chairs. My set is walnut and so is the buffet, but I am bothered by several comments people have made about it being veneered. I wasn't aware at the time I made the purchase that it was veneered, and I would have bought it anyway since I liked the way it looked, but I keep thinking I made some sort of mistake by buying a veneered buffet.

It doesn't need to be refinished yet, and to tell the truth I couldn't have told you it was veneered if someone hadn't pointed it out to me. Is it a bad idea to buy pieces of veneered furniture?

A. Not unless you never want to own a buffet, a piano or organ or many of the dressers that were made during the past hundred years or so. Modern furniture manufacturers have helped discredit veneering, for they have used it to disguise inferior wood and workmanship. Earlier craftsmen, however, employed veneer not to hide something, but to enhance both the beauty and the design of their furniture.

I would go out on a limb (no pun intended) and venture a guess that the framework of your walnut-veneered buffet is made of oak and is better constructed than nine out of ten new hutches and sideboards in furniture showrooms today. Veneer permitted craftsmen to build a buffet that would last hundreds of years, would be beautiful to look at and use, and, just as important, would be lighter to transport and reasonably priced. Were the piece to be made using only walnut throughout, the original cost would have been prohibitive for most buyers.

The highly figured grain pattern on the front of this chest of drawers would not have been possible without veneering. Each half of each drawer is nearly identical to the other, only because the craftsman was able to take several slices of veneer from one piece of mahogany.

To give you an idea how seriously early craftsmen took their veneering, we will often find oak veneer on furniture that is built of fine-quality oak lumber. Craftsmen would first build the piece from the standpoint of structure and then would follow by laying veneer over it in such a way that the aesthetic aspect of the buffet, desk or dresser would be emphasized. Thus veneer freed them from having to favor structure over beauty or vice versa.

The major drawback to veneer is that the glues used to hold it in place are susceptible to water, and once veneer does break, warp or chip it is not easy to repair. As long as it is in good condition, though, and it can remain that way through nothing more than common-sense maintenance, you won't go wrong buying a veneered antique.

An astute buyer won't hesitate to take out a flashlight and crawl under a table to make sure the extenders aren't falling apart or that an improper repair hasn't been made along the way. It can also help you spot important labels, identify veneer and locate signs of potential trouble.

Tip—One of the best ways to identify a tabletop as being veneered as opposed to solid wood is to look underneath. While this may seem awkward in the midst of a public auction or in a major antique shop, it will enable you to know exactly what you are buying. A flashlight will help you determine whether or not the grain pattern underneath the table matches that on the top.

• • •

Once beyond repair, veneered pieces sometimes take strange forms, as illustrated by the following two letters:

Q. I recently purchased from an antique dealer a round oak dining room table for three hundred and seventy-five dollars. It has been refinished and looks very nice. The receipt he gave me with it says "oak table with maple top." Is this unusual, since I have never seen a round oak table that didn't also have an oak top? Do you think I paid too much for it?

A. I don't like to play armchair appraiser, so won't venture an opinion on the value of the table. Since I do have my license to play backseat refinisher, I will toss out my opinion on your "oak table with maple top."

I've yet to see or hear of an antique round table that was manufactured with the intention of having an oak base and a maple top. If the skirt of the table is also oak, then I would surmise that the tabletop once had an oak veneer that was removed and the underlying maple refinished to match the rest of the table. The veneer was probably in bad shape, and rather than go to the trouble and expense of applying new oak veneer, the refinisher chose to turn the oak table into an "oak table with maple top."

If the skirt is not oak, then I would check to see if the all-maple top perhaps came from a different base. By looking underneath you should be able to determine if the base and top were adapted to fit one another.

The dealer apparently did not try to convince you that the table was 100 percent oak, since the receipt mentions the maple top. Had he done so, then you would be justified in returning the table and demanding your money back if you were dissatisfied with it. If the wood is properly identified, then no attempt to deceive the consumer is being made; only when the dealer tries to pass an antique off for something it is not has there been a case of fraud.

Q. At an auction recently I bought what I thought was a medium-sized walnut parlor table. There was so much stuff piled on it that I couldn't get a good look at it, espectially the top, which had several boxes on it, but I bought it anyway. I knew that it had been refinished at some time but not very well, so I knew I would have to strip and refinish it myself. I have refinished several walnut pieces before, so the prospect didn't bother me.

The table has since been stripped, but I'm afraid I was mistaken about it being walnut. The boards around the edge all look to be walnut, but those in the middle have green streaks in them and don't appear to be walnut. Could they be a variety of walnut I haven't seen before or did I buy an expensive lemon?

A. I would guess that the previous refinisher did both you and the table a disservice. The walnut edging and suspicious interior pieces lead me to believe that your table was once veneered. The boards along the sides would have shown, thus they were walnut, but the inside top pieces would have only served as a foundation for the walnut veneer, thus a less expensive wood was used.

The green streaks would seem to indicate that the secondary wood in this instance was poplar, which was often used under walnut veneer. When it was new, your table would have appeared to be solid walnut.

At some time since then the veneer must have come loose and was removed rather than repaired. The refinisher (in this case not a restorer) apparently sanded the poplar, stained it to imitate walnut and applied a finish. The auctioneer or owner may or may not have been aware of this, but it is the buyer's responsibility in the final tally to make sure the piece is what he or she thinks it is, and not a close imitation.

. . .

Switching from walnut veneer to oak, a reader brings to our attention a pertinent question that anyone who has or plans to shop for oak antiques had better be able to answer:

Q. I have what may seem a dumb question, but no one has ever been able to really explain to me what the difference is between red oak, white oak, golden oak and Mission oak. Can you?

A. I can try.

Red and white oak are two species of oak trees. They are naturally very similar in many ways, but white oak has been preferred by furniture makers because it is more durable than red and resists decay longer. Actually white oak is not white, but is either tan or light brown in color. Red oak, however, does display a pinkish cast, especially when given a completely natural finish.

Golden oak does not refer to a particular type of tree, but instead identifies either white or red oak that has been stained or finished in a golden or yellow tone. White oak is used more often than red in furniture that is to be finished as golden oak simply because its natural color comes closer to being golden oak when finished without a stain.

Mission oak refers to a style and not a type of tree. It was popular from 1900 through 1916, during which time much furniture was constructed from red or white oak and either stained or fumed to appear darker than would occur naturally. The Mission furniture style was very rigid and plain, almost to the point of being considered harsh, and featured pegged joints and exposed tenons in the finer pieces.

.   .   .

And while on the subject of Mission oak, which has experienced a sudden surge in popularity in the past decade and has worked its way onto the showroom floors in antique shops that only a few years ago were turning it away, we'll take a look at this letter:

Q. I have a library table that I bought in 1919 when I was just sixteen years old. On the back is stamped the words "Fumed Oak." The table is very solid, very plain and very dark. The four posts are square.

I want to bring it down from upstairs and use it in my parlor, but a friend says I should have it refinished to make it lighter. There is hardly any finish left on it. I don't mind it dark, but if it would look better refinished that would be good. I would appreciate knowing what you think I should do.

A. Fumed oak, as you may know, is not a wood, but instead refers to oak boards that have been exposed to ammonia fumes. The resulting dark coloration is nearly permanent and is little affected by either stripping or bleaching. The Mission-oak movement early in this century used the fuming process extensively, and it sounds as if your library table may be one of these pieces.

You shouldn't attempt to lighten your table or you risk devaluing it. Clean it with turpentine and fine steel wool before doing anything. If it needs more protection, you can either apply a coat of paste wax or brush on one or two coats of varnish. Mission oak pieces have increased in value dramatically the last ten years, with those that bear the manufacturer's mark and still have their original finish intact commanding the highest prices. If you aren't sure how to determine if your table is either a signed Stickley, Roycroft or Limbert piece, check with your local bookstore or library for books on the subject. Several have been written in recent months and are quite accurate in identifying and dating Mission oak furniture.

Although it is easy for us to forget, every style of oak furniture popular today was just as popular—if not more so—almost a hundred years ago. In fact, oak was so popular around the turn of the century that some furniture manufacturers, attempting to capitalize on the craze, returned to a centuries-old process called "graining" to imitate oak grain on furniture constructed from less expensive wood. Today much of this false-grained furniture is still around, as our next reader will testify, and, although it deserves respect in its own right, cannot yet be considered as valuable as the same piece made from real oak.

Q. We have a library table in our family that for years we thought was oak. The finish has begun to flake off recently, so we decided to refinish it ourselves, but when we took a close look at it we discovered that our oak table wasn't oak at all. The grain appears to have been painted on and doesn't match the wood on the underside of the table. Is the table worthless and should we go ahead and strip it?

A. Your table sounds like an example of a technique called graining. It has been practiced for centuries and was not uncommon soon after the turn of the century.

Graining, which was often done to woodwork in houses, was a two-step process. First, a base coat, in the case of oak a yellow base coat, was brushed on and allowed to dry. Over that a grain coat, usually dark brown to simulate the darker grain of the wood, was brushed on. As it began to set up, the craftsman would create a grain effect by pulling a "grainer" through the dark paint.

A grainer ranged in size from 2 to 8 inches wide. It had a handle on one side and several hard rubber protrusions on the opposite side. By changing the angle of his stroke, the craftsman would imitate close-grained quartersawn oak or the wavy grain of plain sawing. After this dried, a coat of clear finish was applied.

Stripping will remove the finish over the painted grain and the graining as well, leaving you with an inferior piece of bare wood. At that point your table will be worth very little.

By preserving the graining, however, you will be saving what has become a rarity today—handcraftsmanship. To restore the

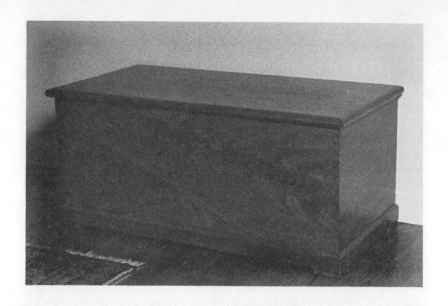

False graining. This blanket box is not mahogany and is not as old as it appears at first glance; the wood is pine, the mahogany grain is hand painted and the chest only dates back to the 1890s. Its value lies chiefly in the fact that the false graining has not been removed.

table, first clean it with a rag dampened with mineral spirits. Be careful not to scrub off any finish that is still intact.

Using artists' oil colors, carefully touch up the spots that have chipped off and left bare wood underneath. When dry, build the finish back up with several coats of shellac and a final coat of varnish. A coat of paste wax will give your table added protection.

False-grained pieces have not been valued as highly as either solid or veneered pieces, but they deserve a better fate than stripping or painting. We may yet see a time when, rather than being shunned, they are sought out by collectors for their uniqueness. Until then, check the insides of the drawers or the underside of the top of any piece you are either considering buying or stripping to make sure the grain on both sides is the same. The difference should be obvious: on the real thing it will be identical; on a false-grained piece it won't.

Q. What is meant by the phrase "a marriage"? I overheard a dealer using it to describe an antique at an auction recently.

A. A "married piece" is one that is actually two or more pieces (or parts of pieces) that were not originally intended to be used together. A common example would be a bookcase added to the top of a drop-front desk or a mirror added to the top of a dresser. Generally a marriage takes place when one of the original parts is missing and the addition of a similar one will increase the remaining piece's value.

Close inspection, though, will almost always lead to the detection of a marriage. In a completely original piece, the two elements should meet perfectly, with no unnatural overlapping. The wood, finish and patina should be identical, as should the wear. Construction techniques and materials should be the same and the entire piece should look natural.

As you may have already gathered, a married antique is not worth as much as the same piece in its original condition, so you need to be on the lookout for them in your shopping. About the only time a marriage is acceptable is when the two pieces have been together for years, and this means more than one or two. If one of our early ancestors took the legs from an oak table to combine with a schoolmaster's podium to make a standing desk, it is still a marriage, but it has a definite value in its own right.

What we need to be conscious of is a recent combination of pieces being sold as original. Marriages don't appreciate in value nearly as fast as originals, so don't be fooled into buying a "great deal" that ends up in a divorce—maybe your own.

. . .

Spotting an incomplete antique is just as important as recognizing a marriage, for unless they are exceptional, any repairs and additions will detract from both the beauty and the value of an antique. (Of course, if your great-aunt left it to you, it's not quite the same as if you went out and bought it, now is it?)

Q. I have a small dresser that was given to me from my great-aunt's estate. It is in excellent condition with the exception that it is missing a strip of wood all the way across the back. Did something special go there or has a board just fallen off?

A. Small dressers and commodes from the Victorian era often came with a variety of different accessories, ranging from towel bars to splashboards to wishbone mirrors. Unfortunately, many of these were taken off, set aside and lost in moves or at auctions.

Splashboards were generally only 5 or 6 inches high and screwed into the space you described with two or three screws. Towel bars were attached much the same way, but heavier mirrors also had slats running down the back of the dresser to help support the weight. By inspecting the back of your dresser you should be able to determine which yours had. You can also compare yours to those in antique shops or at antique shows and, hopefully, find a splashboard, mirror or towel bar that will fit your dresser or have one made at a restoration shop.

• • •

One of the most widely sought-after antiques today are the kitchen cupboards commonly called "Hoosiers." Like most popular antiques, they are well made, come in a variety of styles, are readily available and easily can be adapted to a variety of functions. In addition to being fantastic kitchen pieces, they work equally as well as bars, plant displays, linen closets and china cupboards. The interest in Hoosiers is reflected in a few of the numerous letters we get regarding them:

Q. I would like to know why a cabinet is called a Hoosier kitchen cabinet. We have my mother-in-law's kitchen cabinet that she used in the thirties. One top door has an opening to show where flour was kept, but all the other doors are wood with no glass anywhere. Is this a typical Hoosier cabinet?

A. The term Hoosier cabinet is used rather loosely today by dealers and collectors referring to a style of kitchen cabinets popular from around the turn of the century up into the forties.

There were several different companies producing Hoosier-style cabinets during this period, many of which originated in Indiana, hence the term Hoosier. The most famous of these was the Hoosier Company, and examples of its output still exist in antique shops, shows and auctions.

Hoosier-style cabinets were generally characterized by a two-part construction, the base of which consisted of a silverware drawer, one or two other drawers, a metal mouse-proof bread drawer and a compartment for pots and pans. The top housed a flour compartment with built-in sifter, enclosed shelves for cups and plates and a rolltop to conceal spice jars, cooking utensils and other items.

Illustrating
"Sellers" *Kitcheneed* "Special"
With Automatic Lowering
Flour Bin

This ad for a Sellers kitchen cabinet, one of the type commonly referred to as "Hoosiers," appeared in a national magazine in 1917. Highly sought after, Sellers cabinets exhibit high craftsmanship and innovative ideas. Notice, for instance, the swing-out sugar cannister, the recipe-card holder inside the top door and the ant-proof castors. Original Sellers spice jars can be identified by the S stamped on the bottom of each one.

The top and base were separated by a porcelain counter top that could be pulled out an additional 12 inches for extra working space.

Each company attempted to outdistance its competitors with space-saving devices, additional features (one boasted of its ant-proof castors), popular finishes and lay-away plans. The cupboards have remained a favorite not only with dealers and collectors, but with kitchen enthusiasts as well.

Q. After seeing a Hoosier kitchen cupboard that friends of ours had refinished, my wife and I decided to buy and tackle one ourselves. We were brimming with plans as we loaded our find into and on top of our tiny station wagon, but our glorious plans turned to sludge as we tried to get the paint off our cupboard. The paint didn't come off ours at all like it did off our friends', even after two gallons of the same brand of stripper.

To add to our misery, we have discovered that our Hoosier does not appear to be oak. In fact, it doesn't appear to be any kind of recognizable wood at all. My wife thinks that the dealer who sold us the cupboard played us for a couple of suckers and shoveled off a lemon on us. She says we should take it back and demand our money. Right now I'm more confused than angry. Is there some trick to getting the paint off old Hoosiers? And if it's not oak, what kind of wood do you think it is?

A. You have just learned one of the toughest lessons of furniture refinishing there is to learn—and I know because the first Hoosier-style cupboard I ever stripped was the same type as yours. The wiser among us know that Hoosiers (using the term loosely here to indicate any cupboard of this type) came from the factories in one of two finishes: clear golden oak or painted.

Your friends were either lucky or smart enough to refinish a Hoosier that had originally been a clear golden oak. Even when a coat of paint was put over it, the wood still was oak, and a layer of clear factory finish held the paint away from the pores of the wood.

The painted models, however, often weren't oak and generally didn't receive a coat of clear sealer before being painted. Generally they were a mixture of cheaper woods, such as spruce, poplar, birch and maple, and the paint soaked right in, making it a Herculean task to get it all out.

Depending on how far you have progressed and how you feel

about your Hoosier, you have a couple of options. Purists would insist on repainting your cupboard the same color as it appeared new. Dedicated strippers would plunge ahead, scraping and scrubbing until all the paint had vanished.

When I was younger and more of a dedicated stripper than a purist, I took the plunge and fought the paint. Under it I found four different kinds of wood, but once sanded and stained a light walnut, they blended together nicely. I still use my first Hoosier, for several reasons, one being that it serves as a reminder of all that work. Since then, however, I have been known to turn down similar jobs and to convince people to either repaint their painted Hoosier or sell it and buy a golden-oak variety.

Unless the dealer who sold you the cupboard misrepresented it to you and your wife as being oak or the variety with an original clear finish, you won't stand much of a chance of getting your money back. Hopefully, since it was painted, the asking price wasn't all that much anyway.

Unfortunately, there is no trick to getting the paint off a factory-painted Hoosier. Dipping is dangerous simply because the thin panels and soft woods are susceptible to warping and the backs are almost always veneered. Lye solutions and other extremely caustic strippers are somewhat effective, but dangerous to use. Commercial semipaste paint-and-varnish removers applied thick and left to work to their full potential seem to be the best compromise.

Regardless of your decision, don't discard your original idea. Old Hoosiers, painted or clear, make practical additions to modern kitchens, family rooms or dens, serving as desks, bars, plant displays, bookcases, and believe it or not, even as kitchen cabinets.

_Q_. We have a lovely old Hoosier kitchen cabinet that we actually found in Indiana while passing through on vacation. It was still in its original finish and had the caramel-colored glass in the top of the doors.

We have restored the cabinet completely, cleaning the old finish rather than stripping it and scrubbing the slag glass with a toothbrush and warm water. Rather than try to strip the paint out of the inside of the cabinet, we repainted it the same color as it had been originally (antique white).

When we were painting the inside we noticed two medium-sized screw holes on the right side behind the rolltop curtain. We can make out the faint outline of a missing bracket, but haven't been able to determine what went there originally. Have you seen a cabinet like this one with something there?

A. Many of the top-of-the-line Hoosier cabinets, especially those made by the Sellers Company, came with a swing-out sugar cannister that was attached to the right-hand side.

The cannisters were glass (unlike the metal flour bins) and fit down into an 8-inch ring that, in turn, was fitted into a bracket. The bracket was attached to the cupboard with two #10 screws—thus, your holes.

The sugar cannister could be swung out and a sliding plate pulled to allow the sugar to flow. When not in use, the cannister could be swung back behind the roll.

This convenience probably accounts for its scarcity today, for it would have been easy to break the cannister by roughly shoving it back into the cabinet interior. Some cabinets still have the brackets, but only a few still have the ring and the cannister intact.

Keep looking under tables at flea markets and in the far corners of antique shops, however, for there are still many cannisters out there in need of a new—or an old—home.

Q. I read with interest your reply to the person who has the Hoosier cabinet with the outline of a missing bracket that at one time held a swing-out sugar container.

I, too, have a Hoosier cupboard; mine has a small oak block attached to a sturdy bracket that fastens to the right side, near the front of the upper drawer. It is for attaching a food chopper and I have used it many, many times.

A. Thanks for the information. I recently saw a Hoosier cabinet with two wooden brackets attached to the inside of the back, behind the roll when it is closed. The two brackets only stood out about two inches and were placed a little more than a foot apart. I was not able to guess what purpose they served until the current owner informed me that they were designed to hold a rolling pin! Very appropriate for a piece that was designed especially for baking, I thought, and a perfect place for an antique ceramic rolling pin with an advertising logo on it.

· · ·

In the antique world, value is often affected by quantity as much as it is quality; take, for instance, this situation involving a set of chairs and keep it in mind as you shop:

Q. I bought a set of six oak chairs, very plain, several years ago, thinking I would use them with a table I have. As it turned out I got some other chairs I like better and don't need the set of six. I have three children, all married, and would like to give two of the chairs to each of them. My husband, though, doesn't think this is such a good idea. He says the chairs are worth more as a set. Is this true?

A. It sure is. Let me give you an example, but don't take my prices too literally; they are only meant to illustrate a point.

Let's say that a single oak chair, plain, but in good condition, is worth about twenty-five dollars. Do nothing to it but add another one identical to it and the value of each chair increases to about forty dollars. A third won't help much, but when you reach four, your chairs are up to about seventy-five dollars apiece. And you still haven't done anything to them.

Like the third, the fifth chair won't add much value, because people generally are looking for an even number of chairs. The addition of the sixth chair, however, pushes the value of each chair over a hundred dollars, even though nothing was done except to add more chairs to the first.

I could not advise breaking up the set, for once chairs are separated, even within a family, they rarely come together again. Find which couple has a need for all six, then find something appropriate to give the other two.

Q. I'm looking for a set of chairs to go with a round oak table I was given from my grandparents' estate. I'm rather new to antiques, so don't know for sure what I should be looking for, except that a friend said I need pressed-back chairs.

First, what are pressed-back chairs, and second, is that what would have gone with a round oak table? The table is over 4 feet across, has five leaves, and feet that look like claws. I've been told it is a very good table and quite valuable. I don't intend to sell it, but would like some idea what it is worth. Also, what should I look for when buying chairs for it?

A. In twenty words or less, right?

Your table is indeed a good one. Depending on the section of

Though when they first came out around the turn of the century, pressed-back chairs sold for only about two dollars apiece, they are now one of the hottest items in antique shops. Top-quality chairs, such as the one pictured, featured deep pressed designs, multiple spindles, curved hip rests and caned seats.

the country it happens to be in, it is probably worth between eight hundred and a thousand dollars. Since tables of this type were manufactured from about 1880 up until World War I, the type of chair your friend referred to as pressed back would be appropriate for it.

Pressed-back chairs are so named because of the pattern stamped or pressed into the top piece. There were literally hundreds if not thousands of different patterns produced, and it has become a weekend hobby for some poeple with two or three chairs of one particular pattern to try to find identical chairs to complete their set.

When buying a set of pressed-back chairs, first check to make sure the patterns are identical and not just similar. Sets of four, six or eight chairs are at a premium and will both cost more and be worth more in the future. Second, unless you are willing to reglue them yourself or go to the expense of having them reglued, check to make sure they are sturdy. Nails in joints are a danger signal, for they indicate an improper repair that will make ever regluing the joints difficult. Finally, just as you should never buy a car you haven't driven, don't buy a chair you haven't sat in. If possible, take one home to try with your table to make sure the height and color are both right.

One warning: antique hunting is a chronic disease. You may not have much experience in it now, but once you start looking, you'll be hooked for life.

Q. I found in our family barn a 42-inch square oak table, hanging on the wall. A search turned up four cylinder legs that, except for bird droppings and cobwebs, were in very good condition. I refinished the table and legs, which wasn't too difficult since

Those tremendous round and square oak tables are often held together with just a handful of screws that probably haven't been checked or tightened since about 1913. Unless you want the Thanksgiving turkey in your family's laps you had better turn it over and make sure those screws are all tight.

most of the old finish had disappeared, but now want to have some leaves made for it.

The slides pull out almost forever, and the table will hold nearly eight leaves. I don't think that I want that many, but I'm worried about how many the table can support. I've seen similar tables in antique shops with a fifth leg, but mine doesn't have one. Would it have had one and should it have one now?

A. Yes to both questions. A table designed to hold that many leaves would have had and should have a middle leg (or two) to support the weight of eight leaves, ten pairs of elbows and a twenty-pound turkey.

If you plan to have any more than two 9-inch leaves made, plan as well to have a fifth leg turned and installed. Either way, be sure to tighten the twelve screws that are holding the table extenders to the underside of the top. Right now, they are all that's holding your table together.

• • •

Right along with Mission oak furniture, Hoosier cabinets, pressed-back chairs and square oak tables in the list of "most sought-after antiques" comes brass beds, which were very popular with nineteenth-century Victorians and are enjoying such a resurgence today that companies have sprung up to reproduce old designs. Buying a brass bed requires some additional sleuthing, however, for there were many different types and qualities produced.

Q. I am considering buying a brass bed from someone who is not an antique dealer. He says he thinks it is solid brass, but I'm not sure, and I don't know if he is either. It has been painted, so is there a simple way to find out if it's solid brass without scraping it somewhere?

A. Yes. It is ridiculous to risk damaging any antique with a pocketknife when a small, inexpensive magnet will tell you more faster and easier. Solid brass has no attraction to a magnet; brass-plated steel does. The legs and other weight-bearing pieces will actually be brass-wrapped steel for strength; the dowels and connecting tubes, however, should not attract your magnet if they are solid brass. Make it a point to keep a magnet in your car and you won't ever have to ask if a bed, a piece of hardware or a lamp is solid brass.

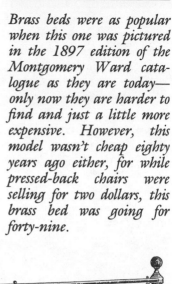

Brass beds were as popular when this one was pictured in the 1897 edition of the Montgomery Ward catalogue as they are today—only now they are harder to find and just a little more expensive. However, this model wasn't cheap eighty years ago either, for while pressed-back chairs were selling for two dollars, this brass bed was going for forty-nine.

No. 650 Brass Bed. The best and prettiest style on the market for the money. Size of pillars, 2 inches; knobs, 3½ inches; top rails, ¾-inch; other rails, ⅝-inch. Height to top rail at foot, 37 inches; at head, 55 inches. Weight 175 lbs. This is a special bargain at our price. Has the swell (bow) foot end.
Size, 4½x6½ feet, only $49.00

Q. I want to find a set of oak stacking bookcases for my husband for his birthday a few months from now, but don't know a whole lot about them. I know they come apart and can be made different heights, but I have no idea what to look for when buying them or how much to pay. Can you give me some advice?

When the Mission style of furniture became popular between 1900 and 1915, even the makers of oak stacking bookcases adapted. This three-section bookcase has the characteristically square look of Mission furniture and features leaded glass panels and a bottom drawer.

A. Stacking bookcases have been very popular since the beginning of the century and are probably enjoying their greatest demand right now. Fortunately for us, thousands were made, so it isn't impossible to find a set in relatively good condition.

To serious collectors the label on the inside indicating the manufacturer is an important consideration, but you need to be aware of it only because then you'll know what additional sections will and will not fit together. Two of the more popular makes were Macy and Globe-Wernicke, although Lundstroms, Gunn and Ginn are also readily available. Each manufacturer had its own style of door hardware, knobs and interlocking system, so keep an eye on labels as you put together your bookcase ensemble.

To be complete, each bookcase should have a removable base and top; the number of stacking sections can range from two to whatever will fit in your house, although four or five are usually considered to be a set. Deluxe models may have beveled glass in the doors or a drawer or two in the base, and a few even came with a drop-front desk section that fit in between two of the regular sections.

Make sure the sliding glass fronts work smoothly and that the laminated backs haven't started coming apart. As far as price is concerned, these bookcases seem to sell for between seventy-five and one hundred and twenty-five dollars per individual unit, depending on condition, style and section of the country.

Tip—Don't depend entirely on any of the dozens of price-guide books now available for an accurate assessment of the value of your antiques. Most are out of date when they finally reach the bookstores, and they can't reflect the range of conditions each antique is found in and don't make allowances for different demands in different sections of the country. Use them to get a general idea, but no more.

Q. I want to buy an oak icebox for our family room, but don't know how much I should expect to pay or what I should look for. Could you give me any indication and some tips on buying? I don't really have a great deal of experience with antiques, but I want to get started.

A. Oak iceboxes are a hot item in almost every part of the country right now and are apt to remain so. Luckily, they were used in every state for a couple of decades or more, thus availability shouldn't pose a major problem regardless of where you live.

Prices vary too widely for me to be much help to you there, for, depending on size and condition, I've seen iceboxes go for as little as one hundred and as much as eleven hundred dollars. Check your local antique shops and attend a few auctions and you'll soon get a feel for prices in your area.

As for what to look for in an icebox, naturally the condition of the inside and your intended use will have to synchronize. Check the top for oil stains and rings from paint cans, as many iceboxes were used in barns and garages after being hauled out of the house.

The most often overlooked damage to iceboxes, though, is wood rot. Many of them stood in water and thus many have bottom boards nearly rotted away. Check them over carefully, for it can be expensive rebuilding the lower portion.

Q. My grandmother left me her Jenny Lind bed when she died, but I wasn't able to use it until now when I have my own apartment. The wood is really beautiful, except I don't know what

kind it is. What I am curious about, though, is why is it called a Jenny Lind bed? Someone else thought it was a spool bed, whatever that is. Can you tell me anything about this bed?

A. The "Swedish Nightingale" made her triumphant tour of the United States upon the arm of P. T. ("There's a sucker born every minute") Barnum during the early 1850s. She so moved her audiences with her singing and her presence that numerous products were named after her, one of which was a style of bed also popular at that time. The spool bed had been so named because its construction resembled a series of spools strung together and, more by coincidence than anything else, came to also be called the Jenny Lind bed.

The style of bed long outlasted the opera singer and, in fact, is still produced today. Because it remained popular for so long, it was manufactured in a variety of styles, woods and qualities, and the range in value of these beds reflects their diversities.

Q. I recently had refinished a chair that had been in our family for years. It is walnut, and the refinisher really did a beautiful job. When I picked it up he referred to it as being Eastlake. I didn't want to appear dumb, so I didn't say anything, but I'm curious. What did he mean by that?

A. An architect by training, Charles Lock Eastlake (1836–1906) is remembered more for his small book *Hints on Household Taste in Furniture, Upholstery, and Other Details* (1868), which greatly influenced furniture design for the next fifty years. Eastlake-influenced furniture is generally made of walnut, oak or mahogany and, though it features simple, functional design, geometrically balanced, it is often highlighted with burl veneer. This particular style reached its zenith in 1876, but has remained popular with collectors ever since.

Q. Could you explain for me exactly what "bird's-eye maple" is and how it is formed? I have inherited my grandmother's bedroom set, which is partially made up of what I have been told is bird's-eye maple, but no one seems to be able to tell me what it is. I want to find some more pieces to add to the set but haven't found any locally. Are bird's-eye maple pieces hard to find and more expensive than regular maple or other woods?

A. Hard maple has been a popular wood among cabinetmakers for centuries, for not only is it strong and attractive, but it responds well to the plane and scraper. Its somewhat scarce and highly desirable aberration, bird's-eye maple, shares these attractive qualities in addition to having a unique appearance.

It is commonly believed that the unusual figuration associated with bird's-eye maple results from young buds being unable to make their way to the surface of the tree. Frozen in place, the tiny buds force the annual rings to grow around them, forming, when sliced by the saw, tiny abnormalities resembling bird's eyes.

(Other theories as to the cause of the "bird's eyes" do exist, tracing their origin to infiltration by insects, fungi or birds pecking out insects with their beaks.)

Since it has always been somewhat scarce, the best bird's-eye maple was generally reserved for veneering, with one choice log thus being able to cover several pieces of furniture. Those who consider bird's-eye maple particularly attractive and seek it out for their collections find prices are often higher than those paid for similar pieces in more common woods. Sleepers can often be discovered, however, lost among piles of Victorian oak and walnut monstrosities and marked far below their market value; so it is definitely worth looking.

Q. As an antique dealer, collector, appraiser and researcher, I would like to level some criticism at some auction houses and dealers around the country. Several of them have advertised rococo furniture recently in national trade papers, and some of the pieces have been erroneously attributed to John Henry Belter.

Auction houses and dealers who label all rosewood furniture as Belter are misleading the buying public into paying more for certain pieces than the pieces are worth. Belter is a magic name in rococo furniture, but all rosewood furniture pieces are not necessarily Belter.

A. Inaccurate labeling and identification of furniture in both antique shops and auction houses is not a new problem for consumers, and it has had long-term effects on the credibility of both dealers and auctioneers.

Buyers can't rely totally on either the dealer's or the auctioneer's knowledge or ethics, even if they have known them for years. Both are expected to know everything about every antique that comes into their shop or crosses their auction block, but realistically that just is not possible. They will make mistakes, some of which will end up working to the buyer's advantage. The dealer or auctioneer who habitually misrepresents his or her antiques, however, should be avoided and thus, it can be hoped, will soon be out of business.

The consumer, though, has to take the final responsibility for his purchases. No one interested in buying Belter furniture—or Hoosier cupboards or oak iceboxes, for that matter—should even make a bid if he or she hasn't determined what to look for and how much the piece is worth. Then, regardless of what the seller may or may not know, may or may not claim, the buyer will emerge unscathed.

Keep one thing in mind as you go out to antique shows, shops, auctions, yard sales and flea markets: with only a little homework you can soon know more about your particular field of interest than any dealer, auctioneer or private seller ever had the time to discover. I've always claimed that every shop, show and auction had in it at least one great deal—*you* just have to be ready (and able) to spot it.

3 / Cleaning Antiques— Age Before Beauty

Ever since the refinishing craze swept the nation back in the sixties and seventies, people have too often assumed every antique they found or bought had to be refinished before it could be used in their homes. Now, however, attitudes have changed, and refinishing is but one option to be considered. Restoration has become the catchword, with preservation of original finishes a top priority with everyone from antique dealers to weekend auction addicts.

Now, the first step in a proper restoration is a cleaning of the existing finish—a step that can best be examined using some of the letters we have received from our readers:

Q. I would like to know what method you use for cleaning pieces before refinishing. A lot of mine come from country auctions and have been on the back porch, in the attic or barn until there is so much dirt on them the finish is almost hidden.

A. Cleaning such pieces is important, but not just to prepare them for refinishing. Actually, the purpose should be to determine whether or not refinishing is even called for.

Dirt, bird droppings and other assorted accumulations can be scrubbed off with warm water and a soft rag. However, don't go hosing down furniture, or tossing a bucket of water over it. Water and wood don't mix, so use more rag than water.

And while speaking of water, if veneer is present and loose go even easier on the water. If you think water and wood don't get along well, you should see what it does to old veneer glues.

Q. I have two questions about an old spool cabinet that we found in a barn on some property we just bought. I think it is made of oak. It has six long drawers and has some labels on the sides. Right now it is still too dirty to tell what the labels say, and I didn't want to do something to hurt the cabinet's value until I could check with you.

Should I refinish it? If I do, what will happen to the labels? Also, one of the knobs was off and in a drawer, so I went ahead and cleaned it with some brass cleaner. It shined up very nicely, but when it dried it turned chalky white. I did it over, and the same thing happened. What can I do to keep this from happening again?

A. You are right in being concerned with the labels on the spool cabinet. Regardless of their condition they should be saved, for they help document the origin of the cabinet and have a direct influence on its value.

Begin by gently cleaning the cabinet with a little soap and water. Wipe dry, then scrub lightly with #0000 steel wool dipped in a solution of equal parts boiled linseed oil and gum turpentine. If the labels don't appear to have a coat of finish over them, switch from the fine steel wool to a soft cloth.

As for the pulls, the chalkiness is dried cleaner you didn't wipe off. To remove it, dampen a cloth with a little lacquer thinner and wipe down the pulls after you have cleaned them. If you want them to stay bright and shiny, get an aerosol can of lacquer and lightly mist each pull before you put it back on the cabinet.

Tip—Beware of home-remedy furniture cleaners. One I heard about actually contained a heavy concentration of TSP (trisodium phosphate), which, as you may know, is used in furniture

Regardless of their condition, old lettering and labels should never be stripped. Spool cabinets especially are dependent on the existence and condition of their labels for a good deal of their value. (Notice the hardware on the bottom drawers—a good example of a bad decision.)

stripping. Stick to commercial cleaners or those recommended by reliable experts and, even then, test them on an inconspicuous part before jumping in.

Q. I have several antiques in my apartment that I have bought at auctions and antique shops. Some I have refinished, some were refinished before I bought them and some are still in their original finish. I've noticed lately that the ones in their old finish are becoming sticky, and it looks like the finish is getting soft, because I can scrape it off with my fingernail. Does this mean that they need to be refinished? I was always under the impression that an antique in its original finish was worth more than one

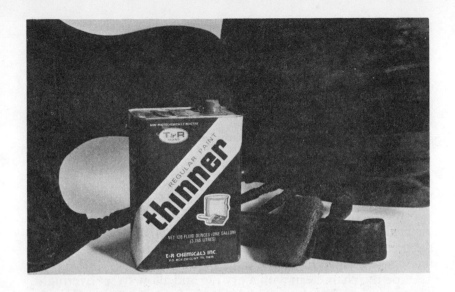

Rather than automatically stripping any antique you buy, first clean it with #000 steel wool and mineral spirits (paint thinner). That will remove the dirt and old wax and will enable you to clearly assess the condition of the finish.

that had been refinished, but how can that be when the old ones are too sticky to use?

A. Good point.

There is, however, at least one other option for a sticky finish besides refinishing. If an old shellac, varnish, oil or lacquer finish has gotten to the point where your guests can't get out of your chairs or your plates stick to your table, a proper restoration (note I didn't say refinishing) can, in fact, increase your pieces' value.

Before grabbing a gallon of paint-and-varnish remover try giving your antiques what we call a clean and polish. Begin by dipping a pad of #000 steel wool in a can of mineral spirits and scrubbing off the buildup of dirt, wax, sweat and whatever else has had a chance to begin growing on your furniture. Afterwards you should be able to determine what the condition of the finish is. If there is still plenty of protection left for the wood, simply polish it with lemon oil. If the old finish disappeared with the wax and dirt, then it is time for some serious restoration—and another question.

Q. I have a set of six stenciled reproduction Hitchcock chairs that have become quite dirty after several years of use. Can you recommend something to use to clean off the buildup of wax and grime that will not damage the stenciling?

A. A formula used by a clock restorer I know has worked quite well in cleaning stenciled furniture. Combine one cup of boiled linseed oil, one cup of gum turpentine, one cup of vinegar and two tablespoons of denatured alcohol in a glass or metal container. Dip a pad of #0000 steel wool into the solution and rub the piece gently. The solution is not highly caustic, and cleaning the wood will require some diligent work.

Wipe the chair clean with a dry rag and allow to set overnight. The next morning buff with a dry soft cloth. To restore the sheen, polish with lemon oil.

Q. I have a lovely old wooden duck decoy that needs cleaning and perhaps something else. The black areas are rather dull and worn. I like them that way, except they are dirty. The white area may have been repainted at some point in time as it is thicker, cracked and slightly peeling.

What should be done to this decoy? It does not have eyes. Is it best to leave it that way or should glass eyes be added?

A. Any loose or obvious dirt can be removed with a sponge and some warm water, while a thorough cleaning can be achieved by substituting turpentine or mineral spirits for the water. Nothing is going to remedy the cracking and peeling of the white areas, so you are going to have to be very careful when cleaning them.

The only touch-ups I would recommend would be where any flakes of paint have come off completely, leaving an obvious mark. Make sure, however, before doing any touch-ups that your paint match is identical, or don't do it at all.

After cleaning, there are several options available to keep both the wood and the paint from drying out. I think varnish would give too much of a gloss to the decoy, so would lean toward an application of paste wax. It will not darken the paint or the wood, but will protect them from further decay.

As for the eyes, I wouldn't put on glass eyes until you can determine from seeing a similar decoy that yours indeed did originally have eyes and until you have found some identical to those previously used.

Q. Upon occasion rather than strip and refinish a piece of good used furniture, I have elected to restore the finish and protect it with a coat of clear varnish.

Last week I picked up a mahogany piano desk, but, after thoroughly washing the piece and touching up some blemishes, I discovered that my protective coat of varnish wrinkled into what looks like a bad case of acne. I suspect that years of commercial polishes have left a film that is causing my varnish to react. If so, what can be used to clean furniture that guarantees the removal of any silicones that may be present, but that will not destroy the existing finish?

A. Probably the oldest existing furniture cleaner is still the best—standard turpentine. It will cut through grease and wax, yet won't dissolve the finish.

Standard procedure is to pour a small amount of turpentine in a glass or can, dip a pad of #0000 steel wool into it and rub the piece gently with the grain to cut through the contaminants; then wipe dry with a clean rag. You can also increase your chances of having your varnish stick to the old finish if you first apply a sealer coat of two parts denatured alcohol mixed with one part shellac. It seems to have better adhesive power and will provide a smooth, clean base for your varnish.

Q. I have a cherry hand-carved lion head that once was on the arm of an early reclining chair. It has a heavy buildup of wax on it that I would like to remove. Will water hurt the cherry wood? What should I use to clean off the old wax? Right now it is very dark. Is there any way I can lighten it?

I have to tell you a funny story about the lion. It has its mouth open and teeth bared. We had it stored behind the couch waiting to be worked on when one day our dog started to go back there. He promptly retreated and has never gone back there since.

A. Bright dog. Maybe he thought he was going to get stuck with the job of cleaning the lion.

Q. I have a set of end tables and a coffee table in Danish teak, purchased about fifteen years ago. I also have a dining room suite in Chinese teak that was purchased about ten years ago. Both of these sets are in need of a good cleaning. What would be the best way to go about this? Both have an oil finish and don't shine very well anymore because of the dirt buildup.

Could you also tell me if there is a difference in the wood of Danish teak and Chinese teak?

A. Just as a rose is a rose, teak is teak. And though Hamlet may have been a Dane, Danish teak doesn't grow in Denmark.

Teak wood comes primarily from Southeast Asia and India and not from either Denmark or China. When furniture manufacturers refer to Danish teak they are referring more to a particular design rather than a type of wood. While I am not familiar with the term Chinese teak, I must assume the same applies.

Teak has a heavy silicate content, making it difficult to either varnish or lacquer. For this reason it is almost always oiled; and after several years and numerous applications of oil it will need to be cleaned. For this I would recommend standard mineral spirits and either very fine steel wool or steel-wool substitute.

After cleaning, give the wood a day to dry, then apply a new coat of Danish oil. I don't recommend boiled linseed oil, because it stays soft and can become sticky in summer. As for the shine, one of the reasons many people like teak is because it doesn't shine—and you'll have a hard time ever getting it to.

Q. On a trip to Europe fourteen years ago my husband and I purchased an 8-foot teak table with two leaves that pull out from either end. With both leaves out it is a full 12 feet in length. We have always tried to be careful in using it since it has an oil and not a varnish finish.

We have noticed that over the years a few dark rings and stains have appeared that resist all our attempts to remove them. A well-known writer of refinishing books suggested using mineral spirits to clean it, but it had no affect on the rings, especially two that appear to be rings from milk glasses. Do you have something to recommend to remove the rings and stains?

A. Guess I wasn't the "well-known writer of refinishing books," huh?

The greatest problem with an oil finish is that the pores of the wood remain open and susceptible to food, dirt and liquids. If the steel wool and mineral spirits wouldn't remove the stains and rings, additional rubbing may be required. Purchase a can of Danish oil and a few sheets of #600 "wet/dry" (waterproof) sandpaper. Tear the sandpaper into fourths and saturate with oil. Keep the paper saturated with oil as you lightly wet sand the tabletop. Keep your strokes light and straight with the grain.

The friction of the sandpaper will remove stubborn stains while the oil will keep the wood from being scratched. Continue to dip the sandpaper in fresh oil as you work along the table. Resist the temptation to just sand the rings, or you will end up with a light area where each was. Wet sand the entire table to the same degree you wet sand the rings.

Wipe off the excess oil and the material loosened by the sanding with a clean rag. Follow the directions on the can as to drying time before buffing. The following day apply a fresh coat of oil, let it soak into the wood, then wipe off the excess, and buff.

. . .

Wood isn't the only antique material that often needs attention. Metals such as brass and copper are often integral parts of our antique furniture and can be quite frustrating to clean and keep clean.

Q. A friend who has since moved to California told me years ago about a recipe she used to clean badly tarnished copper. I am trying to restore an old copper boiler, but none of the products I have found seem to do any good. Do you have any old recipes that might be similar to my friend's? It seems one of the ingredients was vinegar.

A. Try this one: Combine two parts vinegar with one part lemon juice, then add a couple of dashes of salt. Apply with a soft cloth, covering the tarnished area with the solution, then rubbing. Buff with a dry cloth.

Tip—For a quick brass cleaning, dip half a lemon in salt and rub brass briskly. Wipe dry and apply a polish.

Q. I have several pieces of brass and copper, including a brass bed that belonged to my great-grandmother and a copper washtub. I was able to clean off all the tarnish on both these pieces and some

Vinegar, lemon juice and salt—an old recipe for brass cleaning.
It's not the fastest cleaner, but it's the cheapest.

other smaller ones, but every time I check them over I find more
tarnish appearing. What do you recommend to keep copper and
brass shiny after it has been cleaned and polished?

A. I have found two methods, both of which I use with equally
pleasing results. One way to preserve the nontarnished look is to
apply a thin coat of paste wax to the article. Follow the directions
on the can, which will suggest waiting fifteen to twenty minutes
before buffing.

On pieces that are difficult to wax, such as intricate drawer
pulls and handles, I mist the piece with lacquer from an aerosol
can. I stress the word mist, for a heavy coat can run or give your
piece an unnatural appearance. Hold the can 12 to 15 inches
away from the hardware and let the spray fall over it. The lacquer
dries in a matter of seconds and will seal out air and moisture. If
you want to polish the hardware again later, a small amount of
lacquer thinner or varnish remover will melt the lacquer right off.

Tip—Screw heads in antiques should not be overpolished. Cleaning off rust with steel wool is permissible, but don't shine them up with sandpaper or a wire wheel, or they will detract from the rest of the piece.

Tip—One of the fastest ways to clean dirt and grime off chrome- or nickel-plated hardware, such as that found on Hoosier cupboards and old oak iceboxes, is to rub with a pad of #0000 steel wool moistened with a liquid metal cleaner to help keep the steel wool from scratching the hardware.

. . .

Paintings and antiques have always enjoyed a close relationship, but cleaning paintings is far more difficult—and dangerous—than shining up a piece of hardware or an old copper boiler:

Q. I have inherited an original oil painting done by an American artist, Gunther Hartwick. We are not yet sure of its value or whether or not we wish to sell or keep it. Before doing either, however, something should be done to make it more presentable. It is very dirty from years of hanging in a room heated with coal. I have heard that oil paintings can be cleaned and restored without a great deal of trouble. Could you outline the process for me?

A. Although there are several authors who attempt to guide their readers through the oil painting restoration process, I do not feel that it should be attempted by anyone but an experienced professional.

As you will no doubt discover, Hartwick is a much sought-after nineteenth-century American artist. To risk damaging his work with a home restoration would be unjust to both him and yourself. If you intend to sell the painting, take it in its present condition to a reputable art dealer who will be able to assess the value of the painting even through the haze of coal soot.

If you intend to display it in your home, have its condition analyzed by a restoration expert. He or she may recommend a cleaning or a complete restoration, depending on its condition.

Tip—Oil paintings should not be dusted with a cloth for fear of damage to the paint. Instead, take a new, inexpensive paint brush and gently feather dust your painting.

Q. We have a set of Roycroft Mission oak chairs that have been in our family for years. The chairs have never been refinished and still don't appear to need to be. The seats and backs of the chairs are leather and have dried out and begun to crack in places. What would you recommend to clean and preserve the leather?

A. One of the best ways to clean leather is to take a sponge dampened with warm water, wring dry and rub over saddle soap; then work up a lather on the leather with small circular motions. As your sponge becomes dirty, rinse it out in warm water, wring dry and repeat above steps.

Next take a clean, damp cloth and rub the lathered surface briskly. When most of the lather and dirt has been picked up by the damp cloth, switch to a soft, dry cloth for a final buffing. Treat the cleaned leather with a commercial leather dressing. The dry spots indicate that the oil has evaporated out of the leather, and the dressing will help restore it.

Q. I bought from a flea-market dealer a box of old newspaper print block letters. He made me a good deal because he hadn't taken the time to clean them up yet. I think I've found out why, because nothing I've tried will take off both the dirt and years' accumulation of printer's ink without a great deal of work. Any suggestions to keep my good deal from becoming a "turkey"?

A. For small jobs of this sort, I have used cotton balls and a bottle of fingernail-polish remover. It's a perfect project for an evening in front of the television.

For larger and more stubborn jobs, I return to my workbench where I get a can of lacquer thinner, several rags and both a scrub brush and a toothbrush. The lacquer thinner evaporates quickly, so a quart disappears in short order on large jobs. It seems to work the best, however, at cutting through the ink. Since it does evaporate rapidly, you quickly find out whether or not you got off all the grime and ink the first time.

• • •

And if there's one problem we all run into sooner or later with antiques, it's musty drawers:

Q. I recently inherited a walnut Eastlake-style dresser from my great-aunt's estate. The entire dresser, including the hanging mirror and handkerchief drawers, is in excellent shape. The finish is still clear as well. The problem lies in the drawers. The dresser had been stored for years in my great-aunt's attic without being used. This probably accounts for its excellent condition, but the drawers are extremely musty smelling. Is there a way to remove the strong musty odor?

A. It takes years for a dresser to build up a good, strong musty odor and it won't want to give it up easily. There are several home remedies you can try, but don't expect immediate miracles.

First, remove any newspapers or similar material used to line the drawer bottoms. (Before throwing old newspapers away check them over carefully for articles and photographs of historical interest.) Take the drawers, and if necessary the frame, outside and set in the sunlight. The musty odor you are smelling is coming from the wood, and the sun and wind will help draw it out.

If a couple of sessions of sunshine eliminates your problem, bring your dresser back inside and reassemble. Any lingering odor may be absorbed by an open container of baking soda in each drawer. A small bag of cedar chips will also help disguise any lingering odors.

Severe cases may warrant more extensive steps. Sand the sides and bottoms of the drawers lightly with #180 sandpaper, and then brush on a coat of sealer, either shellac, thinned varnish or tung oil. The sealer will lock any remaining odor in the wood and should eliminate your problem.

4/ Removing Old Finishes

As much as we hate to see it, sooner or later we all run into an antique with a finish that simply can't be saved. Regardless of whether it be shellac, varnish, oil or lacquer, when the finish no longer protects the wood or enhances the beauty of the piece, it is time to take action. Before pulling on the rubber gloves, however, and reaching for the goggles and a gallon of the nearest stripper, consider a few of these situations:

Q. Ever since I read in an antique magazine that a good portion of the value of an antique is dependent on its patina, I have been afraid to apply stripper to anything I have bought. Some of my purchases have the finish flaking off or worn down to the wood in places, and I know it will have to come the rest of the way off, but will stripping remove the patina?

A. There are several aspects of a piece to consider before covering it with paint-and-varnish remover, but don't think that you automatically ruin an antique when you replace a ruined finish with a new one.

First, consider whether your purchase is a true antique or simply an older piece of furniture. If it is a unique piece or made around or before the Civil War, do not remove the finish, regardless of its condition, without first consulting an experienced dealer or professional restorer. The majority of the pieces most of us collect and use are not yet true antiques, and when their finishes are as you described, competent refinishing will increase their value.

Second, every antique has two patinas. The wood will have achieved a patina and the finish will have done the same. A good-quality paint-and-varnish remover, applied and used according to directions, naturally will destroy the patina of the finish, but will not affect the patina of the wood. Only rough handling and incompetent use of scrapers, wire brushes and sandpaper will endanger the patina of the wood.

. . .

Stripping is *not* the only alternative to a tired finish; before that, you may want to try following this example:

Q. I have heard the trend now is *not* to remove old paint and finishes from antique furniture. We have purchased an old cannonball rope bed. The finish is dark and crazed. Do we try to clean it the best we can and leave it alone or do as my husband wants and get it refinished?

A. If at all possible, the old, original finish on your bed should be preserved and not removed—and hopefully we can improve its appearance to the point where your husband will be satisfied.

Many of the old finishes can be rejuvenated and the crazing removed by using a solvent such as denatured alcohol or lacquer thinner. Test to see which dissolves the finish by dabbing a little on a rag and rubbing it on the underside of a rail or inside a leg. Either might work, or it might take a combination of both the denatured alcohol (a solvent for old shellac finishes) and the lacquer thinner.

Once you have determined which is the best solvent for your finish, gently rub the bed down with a rag dipped in the liquid. If you rub too hard or for too long, you will remove all of the old

Many pieces of older furniture can be stripped using denatured alcohol, lacquer thinner or a mixture of the two. It's less messy than commercial stripper, isn't as harsh on the wood or your skin and gives you more control over how much old stain and finish you remove.

finish, so be careful. Work on a small area at a time until the crazing begins to disappear, which means the old finish has melted, then leave it alone. The remaining finish will reharden, minus some dirt, darkness and the crazing.

Afterwards, rub the bed down with #0000 steel wool dipped in lemon oil. What you will have then is the original finish restored rather than refinished. You have preserved both the value and the beauty of the bed and, most likely, your husband's high opinion of your refinishing ability.

• • •

As much as I would like to, I can't take credit for that formula for saving an old finish. Several enterprising manufacturers, in fact, took the idea a step further and began offering an alternative to paint-and-varnish remover called "refinisher." It seems to cost as much as stripper and works much like lacquer thinner and denatured alcohol, as this reader's friend discovered:

Q. A friend of mine told me that a well-known product on the market now, which is advertised as being a "refinisher" without being a stripper, is nothing more than denatured alcohol. The refinisher costs about twenty dollars a gallon and denatured alcohol about a third of that or less. Is what my friend said true and, if so, will denatured alcohol work the same?

A. Product manufacturers are reluctant to divulge the contents of their products, so it is impossible to say for sure what is in each of the refinishers.

The refinishers you are referring to act as solvents to dissolve the finish gradually so that it can be either wiped off or respread. Either way, cracking and crazing can be eliminated without affecting the bottom levels of the finish or the stain and filler.

Denatured alcohol and lacquer thinner have been known to achieve similar results for far less money, but you will have to test each on your finish to see if either will do for you what one of the refinishers will.

. . .

When that doesn't work, it may be time to remove the old finish and put on a new one. Sounds easy, right? Well, sometimes the work is easy—or at least easier than trying to decide which brand of stripper to buy:

Q. Being a rather new antique dealer, I find myself dragging home "bargains" no experienced dealer would touch. I have to do a great deal of refinishing and repair work on these gems and need all the help I can get.

Right now I'm having a problem deciding which brand of paint-and-varnish remover to buy. There must be at least twelve different brands on the shelves, and I never know how to decide which is the best. Could you reveal which type you use and where you get it?

A. I stop short of endorsing one brand of paint-and-varnish remover for every type of finish to be removed. When we first opened our shop we purchased a small can of every type of

The only thing more difficult than using a paintand-varnish remover is picking one. Get recommendations from your friends and other refinishers—and when in doubt go with the heaviest can.

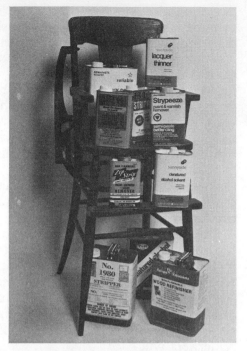

remover we could find and tried them all on different finishes. We still continue this practice today, eliminating several brands from our shop and selecting others for particular jobs.

As a general rule, however, heavy-bodied removers evaporate more slowly and thus work longer than their thinner counterparts. Look for removers with methylene chloride as their active ingredient, for although it, like most stripping chemicals, is harsh on your skin, it is highly regarded by professionals as a solvent for old finishes.

Finally, talk with other refinishers and professional furniture restorers. Some gentle prying might lead you to a remover you haven't had a chance to try.

Tip—If you don't already, consider doing your regluing before you strip off the old finish. The old finish will help keep the glue out of the pores and protect the wood from your clamp pads.

Q. After stripping the paint from a small dresser I rescued from a local junk shop, I discovered that some of the paint had remained in the joints and in several small spots. Rather than put stripper over the whole dresser again, I just dabbed it on the paint spots. Now those areas are lighter than the rest of the dresser. I assume this was not the right thing to do, so what do I do now?

A. Right. What you do to one spot, be it strip, sand, stain or finish, you do to the entire section. If you don't, you get what you've got—spots.

The secret to good stripping is to lay on a thick, heavy coat and then give it plenty of time to go to work. If specks or streaks of the old finish persist, however, brush your stripper over the entire section. It may seem to be a waste of stripper, but it will insure an even appearance. If you don't, you end up with the light areas you described because you gave the stripper extra time to work the color out of the wood.

As for your dresser, a light sanding may even out the spots, but if not, you may need to apply stripper to the entire piece again. Odds are the light areas will not get any lighter, but the parts that only had one strip should.

Tip—If you move your refinishing operation indoors when colder weather descends, don't overlook having adequate ventilation. If you don't, you may someday be standing next to that big dip tank in the sky wondering why you didn't think about the pilot light on the hot-water heater.

Tip—Before brushing on stripper, cover hardware holes and locks on the inside of drawers and doors with several layers of masking tape to prevent drips from spoiling the interiors.

Q. Some time ago a friend of mine, knowing that I restored antique furniture, told me about a homemade stripper that consisted of lye, water and cornstarch, I believe.

Have you ever heard of this mixture, and do you know the amounts that would have to be used? I sure would appreciate finding out the proper measures to use, as a can of household lye only costs about sixty-nine cents.

A. Lye certainly must be the cheapest paint remover and undoubtedly the strongest. However, as far as I know only two types of individuals use it: the brave and the foolish.

As most people know, lye is extremely dangerous. Not only

Any paint-and-varnish remover that is going to destroy an old finish is also going to wreak havoc on both your clothes and your body. Wear proper protective clothing and safety glasses and maybe, just maybe, you'll emerge unscathed.

---

will it burn, blind and maim, it ruins wood. Any antique stripped with lye must be rinsed down with water and then neutralized with plenty of vinegar. If not, the lye will continue to eat away at the wood, the glue and your new finish. Take my word for it, after the lye, the water and the vinegar get done with your piece there won't be much left to refinish.

But I didn't answer your question, did I? Do I know the ingredients and their measures?

Yes.

Next question.

Q. What is TSP?

A. Trisodium phosphate. Bought in crystal form, when TSP is mixed with water it becomes an inexpensive, though caustic, paint remover. It will soften paint in a matter of minutes, but since it has a water base, TSP stripper also raises the grain of the wood, warps thin softwoods and loosens veneer. It is a skin irritant, thus protective glasses, a long-sleeved shirt and rubber gloves must be worn when using it (not a bad idea when using any stripper).

When new and better paint-and-varnish removers became available, the use of TSP declined dramatically, which probably saved the lives of numerous antiques. About all it is used for today is to give stripper rinse water an extra bite—but then do you really want to use water anyway?

Q. Can stripper be saved and reused?

A. Under certain circumstances, yes. Manufacturers will specify whether or not their particular brand of stripper can be used more than once, but generally so long as it has not been neutralized by a rinse agent it can be.

Generally, stripper may be saved after working on large flat surfaces, such as tabletops and leaves, where the stripper can be scraped off easily with a putty knife without benefit of a rinse. The stripper—and the old finish—is then deposited in a metal container until it is used again.

Certain problems can be encountered, however, when using contaminated stripper. Paint and stain dissolved in the old stripper have been known to be transferred to the next antique, adding to rather than reducing your work.

Most refinishers who reuse stripper try primarily to save only that used on old varnish finishes. They then use it for a first strip on heavily painted pieces that are going to require more than one application of stripper. By doing this they avoid contaminating the wood with old finish, for the final strip is done with new stripper.

Tip—When using a putty knife to remove softened finishes, rather than pushing the blade away from you, pull it toward you, handle first. The soft wood scratches easily, but by pulling rather than pushing you can avoid gouging it.

Q. I strip and refinish furniture the hard, old-fashioned way—by hand—but have had many items brought in for me to finish that have been stripped by the "dipping" method.

These items, mostly chairs, small tables, etc., have been for the

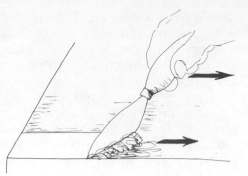

Paint-and-varnish remover will soften not only the finish, but the wood underneath as well. To avoid gouging it with your putty knife, always pull the knife toward you and never push it away.

most part in pieces, meaning most of the glue joints have let go. The furniture is usually brought in a box, and the wood is quite rough, especially oak. People want to know if these pieces can be put back together and made smooth again.

Would it be possible for you to inform our readers as to the differences between stripping by dipping and by hand?

An informative article about stripping would be a great public service and prove to be a source of learning, whether we are pros, weak-end [sic] collectors, avid buyers or just someone who picks up an antique now and then.

A. Much of the controversy that continues to hover around antique restoration has to do with stripping methods and materials. The range of tools is enormous, including everything from jagged pieces of glass to huge dishwasherlike machines, and the assortment can be confusing to pros as well as to weekend collectors.

A dwindling band of misguided disciples still feverishly strip antiques of their old finish with scrapers, both glass and metal. Regardless of their diligence and daring, it's a ridiculous practice. Besides being dangerous to your health, it's hard on the wood. And I'll never be convinced that detailed carvings or even flat-topped desks, for that matter, can be scraped without removing wood; and when you remove wood you remove patina, and without patina you don't have a valuable antique.

Dipping jumps to the other extreme, though care must be taken to distinguish between hot and cold tanks. "Hot tanking," as it is called, involves submerging the antique in a caustic liquid heated well over 100 degrees. Lye or a related villian is most often used, and in addition to eating human flesh it sucks both the finish and the life out of wood. You can generally spot hot-tankers by the patch over one eye or the open sores on their arms.

"Cold dipping" still involves submerging the antique in a vat of stripper, but it is not heated and—hopefully—the stripper is less caustic than lye. Cold dipping is not as traumatic for hardwoods, but it still can be accused of swelling softwood panels and weakening glue joints.

Hand stripping is by far the most often used means of removing an old finish simply because it does not require expensive equipment nor does it present much of a risk to even the finest of antiques. It cannot be denied that hand stripping involves more effort than either hot- or cold-tank dipping, and, if done professionally, may cost a little more, but the risks are reduced dramatically.

Vital to the effectiveness and element of risk of either dipping or hand stripping, though, is the means by which the softened finish is removed. Naturally the skill and judgment of the operator is going to play a major role at this point, but certain methods can be seen as being more harmful than others.

Just as oil and vinegar don't mix, neither do wood and water. Water swells the fibers and makes for additional sanding. No rinse at all, however, leaves a film of stripper on the wood that may contaminate your stain and finish. Mineral spirits, denatured alcohol and lacquer thinner are all more expensive than water, but dry quickly and do not either weaken the glue joints or damage the wood.

To summarize what has been an all too brief answer to your question, choose a method of stripping that is not just cheap or easy, but is safe for you and your antiques.

Tip—If you find yourself out of steel wool in the midst of stripping, an S.O.S. pad from under the sink can save you a trip to the hardware store.

• • •

I can remember asking my grandmother at one time why so much good furniture had been painted. At the time we were in the midst of a giant yard sale, and people were running all over the place, dragging furniture and clothes and old vacuum sweepers back and forth, but she stopped and in the middle of all this confusion told me about how at the time of the Depression all anyone had was wooden furniture, but when it was over many of them wanted to get rid of it because it reminded them of hard times. They still couldn't afford new furniture, she said, so they did the next best thing—they painted it.

So we keep running into commodes and tables and chairs— most of them oak—with layers and layers of paint on them. If we are lucky and the piece still had a good varnish finish on it when it was first painted, most of the paint should come off. If not . . . Well, read on.

Q. Could you pass along some hints on removing paint from deep, intricate carvings? I have a mahogany gentleman's chair with what I think is a beautiful leaf-and-fruit carving along the back. The chair has been painted several times and the carvings are saturated. What can I do to get all the paint out?

A. Try following this plan:

First, don't skimp on the paint-and-varnish remover. Buy a good-quality remover, lay it on thick and walk away. Give the remover time to seep down through the many layers of paint; if it starts to dry out, brush on more.

When the paint starts lifting, bringing up your remover with it, gently scrape it all off with course steel wool. At this point your stripper isn't doing any good since it is no longer in contact with the next layer of finish.

Next pick out the worst of the paint from the crevices with a pick or awl. I don't recommend using a wire brush, for it is liable to scratch the softened wood. Do not rinse the wood yet, however. Instead, apply another heavy coat of stripper. Keep repeating this process until all of the paint and the original clear finish are softened all the way to the wood.

Once again, attack the old paint with your steel wool, but this time use a rinse. Lacquer thinner, mineral spirits or denatured alcohol are more expensive than water, but better for the wood. The only advantage to using water in this one particular instance is that for most refinishers it is the easiest to pressurize, and that is the secret to getting paint out of carved designs: pressure.

Just a little bit of pressure at this point will literally blow the remaining bits of paint out of the carvings. If you have access to an air compressor, you have it made. Otherwise you may have to resort to a garden hose and nozzle, but be careful; water isn't the key, pressure is. Keep your water down and your pressure up.

*One of the more foolish things you can do when stripping finishes—
especially paint—is to begin scraping or scrubbing off the old finish
before the stripper is done softening it. Wait until you can see the
old finish bubbling up under the stripper before you dig in. The
more work you let the stripper do, the less is left for you.*

Warning: I do not recommend this procedure for fragile carvings or for any veneer. The air and water pressure can quickly do
as much damage as good; in the hands of an inexperienced refinisher I have seen it actually disintegrate old veneer and blow
trim across the room.

In addition, it is guaranteed to make a mess of whatever area
you are working in. Bits of softened paint and varnish will stick
to everything and then dry, making it difficult—if not impossible—to clean them up.

Finally, don't wait to pick out those few remaining specks of
paint. Get them while they are still soft, for by tomorrow morning they will be as hard as they were yesterday.

Remember: every minute spent stripping will save you ten
sanding.

Q. I wonder if you have any suggestions as to how I might remove white paint from the pores of a light oak table. After being stripped of several layers of the messy stuff, the piece still shows paint in some of the grain. Sanding doesn't seem to work nor does my friend's suggestion—covering it with varnish and then restripping it. He said he had read where doing that would pull the paint out of the pores, but it didn't. Any suggestions?

A. You must certainly have the stamina of a long-distance runner to have stripped, sanded, varnished and restripped a painted oak table. Most people, myself included, would never have had the courage to start or the perseverance to continue.

At this point I can only think of one alternative and it borders on the drastic. Give your table yet another heavy coat of stripper and enough time for the paint in the pores to be softened. Then take a brass-bristle brush and *carefully* scrub the table, taking care to make sure you go with the grain. It makes a mess of you and everything else around the table and it takes any remaining filler right out of the wood along with the paint, but your table should come clean.

After a thorough rinse, you'll find that the soft pores will have become small canyons. Only an application of paste filler will level out your surface to where you can apply your finish, but it will also cover any deep flecks of paint lurking down in the bottom of those canyons.

To most people that may seem like a lot of work, but I've got the feeling it won't bother you a bit.

Q. I bought a lovely old pie safe from an antique dealer in town. It was painted, but part of the deal was that he was to strip it for me. He did a good job, but just to be safe I stripped it one more time when I got it home.

I sanded it and started putting on a light walnut stain, but when I did, spots of paint started showing up. I couldn't see them before I put the stain on, but now they look terrible. Do I need to strip it again?

A. After two strips, I wouldn't think so. The problem isn't a reflection of your ability to strip off paint, but of the absorbing power of the mixture of hard and soft woods used to make pie safes.

What little finish was originally put on them didn't keep all of the paint from seeping into the pores, joints and cracks. About the only thing you can do is to sharpen an awl to a fine point and begin scratching out the remains of paint. There is no slower process in antique restoration, but the reward is worthwhile.

Tip—Deep gouges, cracks and nail holes have a way of holding a good deal of paint. Rather than making a molehill out of a mountain, patch them with wood dough the color of your stain.

Tip—Get into the habit of laying all used refinishing rags, regardless of what you think is on them, outside to dry at the end of each refinishing day. No sense in burning down the house, is there?

Q. My husband and I are refinishing an old Hoosier cupboard, but unless you can help us figure out a way to get all the old paint off, we may end up in divorce court. We found it in the basement of the house we bought and decided to refinish it and use it in our kitchen. Our big problem is getting the paint to come off— or, as my husband puts it, getting the paint remover to stay on.

A friend of ours who has done a lot of refinishing recommended that we buy a gallon of the cheapest stripper since they are all basically the same. We brush it on, but it runs down the sides faster than we can either brush it back or scrape it off. It isn't working at all on the sides, and even on the top not all the paint comes off. Can you help us, or should I give my husband the cupboard in the settlement and ask for the car?

A. Keep both, but get rid of your amateur expert with the bad advice.

All paint-and-varnish removers are not the same and some of the cheap ones are terrible. (I'd like to mention a few names, but my attorney gets real nervous whenever I threaten to.) Buy the best and, in the long run, you'll spend less money.

Your "friend" should also have known that stripper always works better on horizontal surfaces than vertical. Take your Hoosier apart and strip in steps, turning each piece as you finish so that you are always working on a flat surface. And keep in mind that you don't brush on stripper as if you were brushing on varnish. Lay it on thick and leave it alone.

It's sort of like marriage—the less you mess with it the better it works.

Q. Could you tell me how to get buttermilk paint off various woods? I have tried all kinds of paint-and-varnish remover without success.

I am not sure if that is the correct name of the paint, but an old-timer said it was. I've found it on hickory, walnut and oak and haven't been able to get it off any of them.

A. This old-timer says "If it won't come off, leave it on."

The trend of automatically stripping antiques down to clean wood has begun to diminish now that collectors and dealers have started looking for pieces still in their original paint. "Buttermilk" has become a generic term for many similar paints, some of which were made with milk, others with organic dyes and even animal blood.

Fortunately most of our modern removers don't even seem to dent buttermilk-type paints. What that means is that if you find an antique with numerous layers of modern paint, you often can carefully strip them off and preserve the original buttermilk paint underneath.

What I would suggest, then, for any piece you find in its original finish is cleaning the buttermilk paint with mineral spirits and sealing it with paste wax. You may not get to see the hickory, walnut or oak, but there are a lot more examples of them around than of buttermilk paint.

. . .

And finally, for those of you who jumped on the polyurethane bandwagon a few years ago and have now decided you don't like the looks of it, there's this reader's question:

Q. What is the best means for removing a modern polyurethane finish?

A. A good quality paint-and-varnish remover and lots of it.

Polyurethanes have a way of soaking up stripper, so don't start scrubbing it down with medium steel wool until it is loosened all the way to the wood. After the first coat is absorbed, slop on another. It gets expensive, but otherwise you end up with part of the finish still on the wood when you start sanding—and sanding is bad enough without making it any worse.

5 / Surface Preparation

Wouldn't it be nice if we could just strip an antique, make a few passes with a piece of sandpaper and then lay on a satin-smooth finish—all in about forty-five minutes? Doesn't quite work that way, but that's alright. You certainly wouldn't want to do much antique restoration if you didn't enjoy it, so time shouldn't pose that much of a problem.

Once in a while, however, the wood does—rough spots, dents, rings, holes and other assorted minor ills demand some attention before we can start thinking about putting on a finish. Sometimes we're tempted to let a few of them slip by, but remember, your finish won't hide them. In fact, think of your finish as a magnifying glass—what looks not-so-bad before, looks horrible afterwards. So read on before reaching for that brush:

Q. Could you please attempt to clarify the confusing situation (at least for me) surrounding the different grades of sandpaper? Some woodworkers and books talk about coarse, medium and fine sandpaper, while others talk in numbers like #180 and

#220. Sometimes, too, I'll see references to numbers like 3/0 and 6/0. Surely some of these must be the same?

A. Fortunately for us they are. The differences are mainly types of classification too detailed to be of any real concern to us. Although there is room for argument in the cross-referencing I am going to provide here, this should serve as a basic guide.

Coarse grit is the same as #50 and #60, and is also referred to as 1 in the last symbols you mentioned.

Medium grit is the same as #80 and #100, and is also referred to as 1/0.

Fine grit is the same as #120 and #180, and is also referred to as 3/0.

Very fine is the same as #220, and is also referred to as 6/0.

Technically, there are nearly two dozen different grits of sandpaper, but all that we need to know are the very basics. Besides, refinishers—at least, smart refinishers—don't do very much sanding. And wouldn't be seen with anything coarser than a sheet of #120!

Tip—Sandpaper will only drive pencil marks deeper into the pores of the wood. Use the eraser to remove them—it's not just there for mistakes.

Q. My husband and I do all our own refinishing and have for several years, although in the past several months we have found ourselves having pieces professionally stripped before we start on them. It isn't that we dislike stripping, but we don't like the mess and the fumes that come with it.

Our working arrangement is really quite suitable. My husband makes any necessary repairs and does all the sanding. I take over at that point and do the staining and refinishing. One reason this arrangement works so well is that he doesn't have the patience for working with paste filler, sanding sealer and several coats of varnish, all of which I let dry for several days between coats and then hand sand with #400 sandpaper.

One problem has cropped up recently that has left me a bit confused. As I was brushing the first coat of sanding sealer onto a walnut parlor table we picked up at a used-furniture shop I started noticing tiny curlicues running across the tabletop. I've never seen anything quite like them before, but they're all connected together and nearly invisible until you look for them.

My husband acted a little strange when I showed them to him, but didn't seem to know why they suddenly appeared. I checked some of the other pieces we have done and didn't find them on any of them, so, as I said, I'm a bit confused. Have you ever run into anything like this before?

A. I don't know if you're referring to your husband or the curlicues, but the answer to both is yes.

Someone—who shall remain nameless—has slipped a power orbital sander into the workshop and used it on your tabletop. The tiny scratches you described are left when a lazy wood-worker gets in a hurry and uses something less than very fine sandpaper on an orbital sander. The delicate grain of walnut can't withstand the swirling action of medium sandpaper, but the scratches don't show up until you put on that first coat of finish.

As you may have guessed, you—or someone who shall remain nameless—are going to have to restrip the table and then sand off the tracks left by the sandpaper. As it oftentimes happens, those labor-saving devices can lead to more labor than they supposedly save.

Tip—Don't be in a hurry to grab the belt sander just because your tabletop has several stains in it. Some light hand sanding followed by bleaching with either household bleach or oxalic acid could well restore the top without removing a great deal of wood—and valuable patina.

· · ·

As anyone who has worked around or been around antiques knows, excessive sanding can destroy much of the beauty and the value of a good piece. All that should ever be required is a light sanding to remove the thin layer of stripper residue left after it dries and to erase shallow scratches. If you are accustomed to working with new wood, then you are going to have to get used to the fact that old and deep scratches are a part of antiques; we would much rather have a mahogany dresser with a few old scratches than we would one that looks like it is brand new.

The only sandpaper you should normally need, then, are sheets of #120 for first sanding of oak and ash; #180 for all-purpose sanding and #220 for woods as delicate as walnut.

If, then, you are faced with what appears to be a major sanding project, choose one of these two options: go back and strip it again or read further:

Q. I have an oak hutch that has some black streaks on it left over from when our roof leaked. The insurance company is going to pay for part of the damage, but I am going to refinish the hutch myself. Before I start I want to know what is going to take the stain out of the wood. Do you have any suggestions?

A. Sorry to hear about the roof. Lets hope that a good bleaching will take out the stains that it let in.

After you have stripped your hutch of the old finish, turn it so that the area to be bleached is horizontal. Sand lightly to remove the stripper residue and to open up the pores. Wipe off the dust and then run a double strip of masking tape around the outside edge to hold the bleach just on that one side.

For the bleaching itself use standard household bleach. It has already been diluted and any further diluting will just slow down the process. Brush on a liberal coat and then let it sit. Thirty minutes later brush on another coat and then let it sit overnight. The next day you can sand the piece to remove any fuzziness caused by the bleach, and your stain should have disappeared.

. . .

If household bleach does not prove to be strong enough for your stains, you do have yet another alternative (anything but a lot of sanding!):

Q. I bought a round oak table with claw feet at an auction recently and intend to strip and refinish it. My problem is that it has big dark blue rings on the top that look like ink stains. How can I remove them? Do you think sanding will do it? I wanted to find out what to use before I put any stripper on it.

A. Dark rings can be a source of trouble, but hopefully we can get them out without having to resort to excessive sanding.

Strip the old finish off first so that you can see just how serious the rings are. If you are lucky, some of them will disappear with the old finish. Those that remain will need special attention.

After the table dries, sand it lightly to remove stripper residue. Then dissolve oxalic acid crystals (available at drug stores) in half a cup of warm water until the mixture reaches a point of saturation.

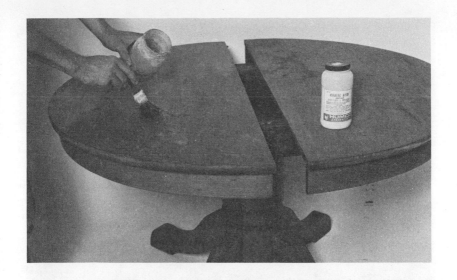

Drastic stains call for drastic measures, but, relax, oxalic acid isn't as dangerous as it sounds. Wear safety glasses, though, as you brush a solution of warm water and oxalic acid crystals on the wood. Cover the entire section, but give the stains an extra dose.

Twenty-four hours later your table will resemble the Great Salt Lake Desert . . .

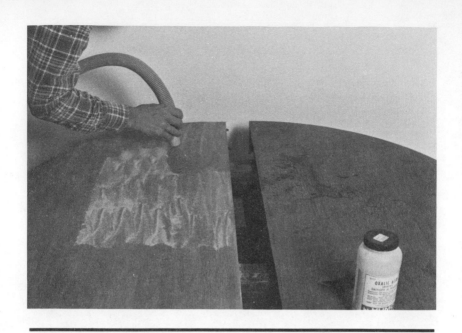

. . . which you should vacuum off while wearing a particle mask, for the crystals can—no, will—cause coughing and sneezing.

Keep your mask on while you sand the table one more time, giving you a top that looks considerably better than it did the day before.

Coat the entire tabletop, but give the rings an extra dose. Take care not to splash the solution on other parts of the table or yourself. The solution will not normally burn your skin, but it is considered an irritant and may cause you some discomfort if you are sensitive to it. Wear safety glasses, however, for like most of the materials used in refinishing it will damage your eyes if you get it in them.

After the oxalic acid dries, put on a dust mask and gently vacuum off the dried crystals. These can cause sneezing and coughing if inhaled, so be careful. You can then begin light sanding, but keep the mask on to keep the dust out of your lungs.

We'll hope that the oxalic acid will bleach out the stains, because excessive sanding will remove the patina of the wood along with the stains and will leave you with an old table with a new-looking top. Don't reach for your sanding block until you've bleached the table at least twice—there's more chance of endangering it through too much sanding than too much bleaching.

Tip—To judge just how serious stains in old finishes are, keep this general rule in mind: white rings are in the finish, black in the wood.

. . .

Stains, then, we can handle with either bleach or oxalic acid, but there are a few other common problems we can expect to encounter sooner or later. Here's one the Surgeon General didn't consider when he scolded the tobacco industry:

Q. I don't know if you've purposely avoided it or if no one has ever written about it, but I've never read how you handle cigarette burns in antiques.

I've got a rolltop desk that, when I start refinishing it, I know I'm going to have to have a good solution to a bad burn problem. I've also got a new coffee table that I don't want to refinish, but it has one long cigarette burn in it, too. Is there a way, other than refinishing, to handle it?

A. Let's take the easy one first.

Hopefully, you'll find that when you strip the finish off your rolltop, most of the burn damage comes off as well. What is left should be carefully scraped away with a single-edged razor blade. Minor burns can be taken care of this way without any extra treatment, but difficult cases will require some additional work.

A hobby knife with a sharp blade is a necessity for cutting out bad cigarette burns. Patch with a piece of veneer of the same type of wood with a similar grain pattern.

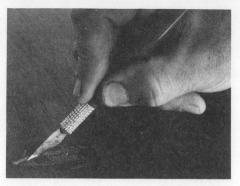

If the burn is deep you are going to have a depression to fill after you clean out all the charred wood. You can choose from three materials designed to build up missing wood: melt-in sticks, wood dough or wood.

Melt-in sticks come in a variety of colors, as does wood dough, but neither matches wood grain as well as actual wood. I prefer trimming a thin piece of wood or a slice of veneer to fit the crevice, gluing it in and sanding it flush later. Some see that as extra work, but the result is far more satisfying than with the other two alternatives.

Q. Would you explain for me the difference between wood dough and wood putty? How do you decide which to use?

A. Basically, wood dough dries and hardens, whereas wood putty will always remain soft. Both come in a variety of colors, but serve two different, though similar, purposes.

Most refinishers use wood dough to repair cracks and holes in wood, which they will later sand and finish. Since wood dough shrinks when it dries, it is mounded slightly over the damaged area. Although it begins to dry right away, twenty-four hours should be allowed before sanding.

Wood putty does not require sanding, thus it comes in handy for filling small holes in furniture you are not refinishing. Since it does not harden, it is not as permanent as wood dough, but can work minor cosmetic miracles on pieces that already have a good finish, but are plagued with a small hole or split.

Tip—A few drops of lacquer thinner (or fingernail-polish remover) will revive wood dough that is beginning to harden prematurely in the bottom of the can.

Q. I have a small oak library table that my father gave me when he retired from teaching. The finish looks as if it is nothing more than several coats of varnish, but it needs to be redone since it has several runs in it.

The only real problem that I can see I am going to have is with a large gouge in the right front corner of the top. I'm not skilled with power tools, and I don't really think the gouge is deep enough to warrant paying a refinisher to put in a wood patch, but it is too bad just to leave alone.

I've used wood dough before, but I'm afraid that it will stand out worse than the gouge itself. Is there some way to help blend it in with the wood or should I leave it the way it is?

A. Wood dough is a great aid to the refinisher, but certainly does pose problems in blending.

On woods such as oak and walnut that have a distinct grain pattern, a large wood-dough patch can appear bland. To give it character, let it dry thoroughly before sanding flush, then use the tip of a hobby knife to imitate the grain of the wood running across the patch.

Don't pretend that the stain you use on the wood will look the same on the patch. An inexpensive package of artists' brushes (or the end of your finger) should be on hand to touch up the patch with drops of various colored stains until it blends in with the wood.

The combination of imitation grain lines and touching up the patch can make wood dough as invisible to the untrained eye as humanly possible.

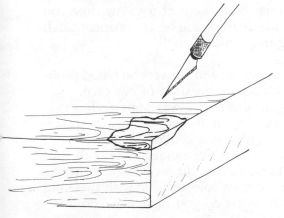

An otherwise bland-looking wood-dough patch can be blended in with the rest of the wood by cutting grain lines in the dried and sanded patch with a hobby knife. Use oil paints to duplicate the color of the wood.

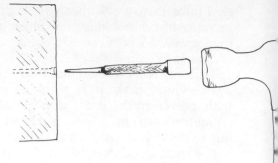

Nail heads are unsightly and should be countersunk ⅛ inch below the surface of the wood. Fill hole with either wood dough or wood putty.

Q. I am trying to save an old table I found in the basement of the house we recently bought, but am unsure of the right way to fill several large holes left in the top. It looks like someone had pounded nails in it. Any suggestions?

A. Small holes can be filled using wood dough, a soft, pliable substance that comes in several different colors. Choose the color that comes the closest to what the table will look like when it is finished; avoid "natural" unless your table is extremely light, for wood dough does not take a stain well.

Larger holes should be plugged with wood. Drill the holes out to the next largest standard dowel size and tap in a length of glue-coated dowel. On maple tables you can use standard dowels from hardware stores, but on oak, walnut and other woods it would be best to cut a plug from the same type of wood.

In either instance, let the plug protrude ¹⁄₁₆ inch above the top of the table and sand it down flush the next day. Anytime you have the choice, use actual wood, for it will be a permanent patch and will be less distracting than wood dough.

Q. We enjoy reading your questions and answers on wood problems very much and now we have a question of our own.

We have a very old plant stand that was apparently made before the wood was completely cured, because now there are two long splits in it. We stripped it and filled the cracks with natural wood dough. The next day we sanded it smooth, but when we stained the top light walnut, the wood dough hardly changed color, so we have a walnut-colored table with two long light strips going through it. What do you suggest we do now?

A. Unfortunately, problems between fillers and stains always seem to crop up. The solutions, however, aren't so easy.

Regardless what its name implies, "natural" wood dough seldom is called for in antique repairs. You are better off picking the color of wood dough that comes the closest to the color the wood is going to be after you stain it. For instance, even though your stand was light after sanding, you should have filled the cracks with walnut wood dough. For twenty-four hours it would have looked strange—two dark streaks running across a light top—but just as soon as you stained the wood the two streaks would have blended in.

You have two options available now: one, you can take a cotton swab or splinter of wood and lay a coat of dark stain just over the filler in hopes that it will absorb some more stain and come closer to matching the wood. The trick is keeping the stain off the wood; hint: use masking tape.

Your second option may sound tougher, but is the correct way to fill splits. You would have to begin by—and you're not going to like hearing this—digging out your natural wood dough and

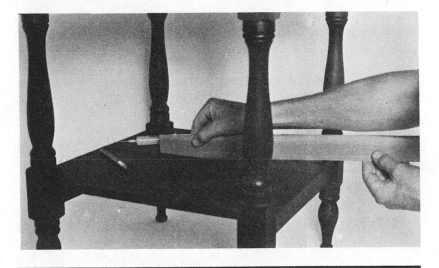

A strip of veneer should be glued into any splits that are a result of shrinkage. The syringe is used to inject glue into the crack, the veneer is inserted and clamped and then, the next day, is trimmed flush with a razor blade or hobby knife.

filling the split with a strip of wood instead. Once glued in and allowed to dry, it can be sanded flush and stained nearly identical to the rest of the wood in the stand.

Q. I have been experimenting with making my own filler for small holes, using sawdust and white glue, but keep having problems with the filler turning white after it dries and is sanded. What causes this and how can I avoid it?

A. All fillers, natural and synthetic, leave something to be desired and the old sawdust-and-glue formula is no exception. It is a good solution, however, so is worth experimenting with to attempt to perfect.

I would guess that the whiteness you are experiencing comes from too much glue in your mixture. Dilute your glue with an equal amount of water (the old-timer who showed me how to mix sawdust and glue used to spit in it—his chaw of tobacco worked perfectly for filler going into walnut) and add only enough of it to the sawdust as is needed to hold it together.

Tip—Add a drop or two of the stain you are using on your wood to your wood dough (or sawdust and glue) before you pack it into the hole or split. It should help blend it in.

Q. I have an old oak kitchen table that my parents gave me for my apartment. I plan to refinish it eventually, but right now I just need to know what to put in the cracks between the boards where the old filler is chipping out. One night while she was studying, my roommate sat and picked out all the old dry filler with her pen, so I need something to put in there until I refinish the table. Can you tell me what to get?

A. How about a new roommate?

Seriously, what you do need is wood putty. Get it in whatever color matches your table best, pack it in with the tip of your finger and wipe off the excess. Wood putty doesn't harden, but remains soft so you don't have to sand it later. That also means that your roommate can sit and pick it out again—if she's still around.

Q. I bought a round oak table sight unseen from a friend of the family. I had remembered the table from countless meals in her home when I was a child and had always admired it. She was asking far less than its market value and had stripped it herself as well. What she forgot to mention was that she had stripped it four years ago and then left it in an unheated garage.

I borrowed a pickup truck, and a friend helped me get the table out of the garage and home. Once I got the dirt and the cobwebs off it, I could see that it had dried out and was covered with hundreds of tiny cracks. Most are at the ends of the boards and don't go very far, but a few are more serious. How should I go about fixing them?

A. Many good antiques have suffered terribly from being stripped with not much more than good intentions. It is a tough way to learn that anything stripped has to be finished soon after.

The large splits should be patched with strips of thin wood or veneer. You can try to clamp them together, but don't expect much success. Once wood has shrunk, it's awfully difficult to get it back.

The hundreds of tiny cracks can be filled with a heavy application of thick paste filler. It can be obtained at most paint and hardware stores that carry refinishing supplies. If you plan to stain the table you will want to add some stain to the filler, which usually comes in a neutral color. Play it safe, though, and read the directions on the can.

. . .

Mention paste filler around a group of refinishers and watch half of them sheepishly slide away. There's no way around it, applying paste filler is messy, hard work—but it's the only way to

If you have a board or table leaf with a bad split in it, you may need to glue in a sliver of wood to fill the gap. Allow the sliver to protrude while the glue dries and then sand it flush with the wood.

get a perfectly smooth finish on open-grained woods such as oak, ash, mahogany and walnut. It comes in a light color and must be tinted and thinned with an oil-based stain to the consistency of thick cream. You brush it across the grain, let it set up and then, just before it dries, scrub it off. The idea is to remove the extra paste filler from the surface of the wood, but to leave it in the pores. Later you sand lightly and continue with your finishing.

Like all restoration steps, paste filling can lead to a few problems, like this one, for instance:

Q. I am a semiprofessional refinisher and have a small drop-leaf mahogany end table in my shop now that a customer of mine brought in. Her late husband made this table several years ago, but now it shows evidence of daily use and needs refinishing. The legs look just like they did when they were new, so we decided to leave them alone.

The problem I have run into involves paste filler. The mahogany never had a stain and is quite light. The pores, though, are dark, and the stripper pulled out most of the old filler. I have to use a filler, but to make it dark, I need to add stain to it. If I do that, however, the wood will soak up some of the stain in the filler and turn darker than the legs. How can I apply dark paste filler without staining the wood?

A. In a similar situation, I discovered that by applying a thin coat of sealer over the bare wood, I could prevent the stained filler from affecting the color of the top. The sealer will not fill the pores, thus the filler (applied after the sealer has dried) will still have something to fill.

After the filler has had twenty-four hours to harden, sand the tabletop with #220 sandpaper and apply another coat of sealer. Finish later with varnish. The color should not be affected and your top, your legs and your customer should all look fine.

Tip—Cut back the bristles on an inexpensive paint brush to about an inch and it will work better for forcing paste wood filler down into the pores of the wood.

Q. I am preparing to embark upon my first true antique refinishing project, a medium-sized walnut drop-leaf table, but am hesitant when the subject of staining comes up. It may sound silly, but how do you decide whether or not to stain a piece?

You'll find that an inexpensive brush with the bristles cut back to about 1 inch in length will be best for working paste filler down into the pores of wood. Brush across the grain to force the paste into the narrow grooves.

A. Your question is anything but silly, and the decision as to whether or not you should stain a piece deserves the serious consideration you are giving it. Antique collectors cringe when they come upon a fine antique that has been damaged not through hard use, but by unnecessary or improper staining.

The most prevalent reason for staining is to achieve a desired color. If the wood is too light for your taste or decor, staining can help remedy the situation. Keep in mind, however, that you are but a temporary owner of each particular antique, and you owe it to both the piece and its future owners not to stray into the excesses of poor taste.

In addition, stains can be used to blend different colored woods together or to help disguise unattractive signs of use. On woods that have lost a great deal of their color through natural bleaching, a light stain can help restore their original tone and highlight their grain patterns. As an example, many people prefer oak with a light walnut stain applied to it rather than left completely natural.

Restoration work of any kind, including staining, should not attempt to change a piece's appearance simply for the sake of change, but should work toward recapturing its original and intended beauty.

Tip—To prevent end grains from absorbing too much stain and thus turning dark, coat first with shellac diluted with denatured alcohol. Let dry and sand lightly, then apply stain.

Q. I would like to share some of my experience in relation to golden-oak finishes. I am a piano technician and collect antique phonographs, pianos, reed organs and players. Many of these have a label somewhere identifying the finish as "golden oak." Always the grain of the oak is accented with a dark filler.

Just staining a piece of bare wood with golden-oak stain will not give the type of finish originally described as golden oak. If you want a real old-time golden-oak finish I would suggest a golden-oak stain which, when dry, should be sealed with a thin sealer. Follow this (when dry) with a dark paste filler to accent the grain, followed by another coat of sealer and a clear finish.

Look over your next oak piece and then experiment with the idea of accenting the grain in a dark tone. I think you'll find it looks much more like an original antique.

A. Excellent point. I think some people have been turned off by golden oak that is actually what I call "schoolhouse oak"—almost pure yellow with no contrasting grain filler. As you said so well, original golden oak had dark pores to accent the piece and was not simply finished in straight golden-oak stain. Thanks for your letter.

Tip—Each can of stain has at least three different color tones in it. The lightest will be at the top, a more medium tone will be in the middle and the heavy pigments will be lying on the bottom. Don't stir the stain until you are sure how dark you want your wood to look. Begin with the tone at the top of the can, test it on your wood; if it is too light, stir the stain gently and test again. Only when you are sure you need a darker color should you stir it vigorously.

Q. I recently stripped and sanded an oak table and four chairs that we bought at an auction last summer. I haven't done anything else with them because I am not excited about the prospect of staining each and every one and then the next day starting over and varnishing each and every one. I've heard about a product called a varnish-stain that is supposed to do both in one operation. It sounds too good to be true. Have you tried it and would you recommend it?

A. Things too good to be true usually aren't. And varnish-stain is no exception to the rule.

Just as stripping and sanding are two different operations, so are staining and varnishing. If you attempt to do both at the same time chances are you'll end up with less than satisfactory results.

In a varnish-stain, color pigments are mixed in with the varnish. Rather than soaking into the pores of the wood, the stain dries suspended in the varnish. As you can no doubt imagine, this leaves you with a finish we call Mississippi Mud.

If you have invested time and money in a good set of furniture, why ruin it with a shortcut at the end? Buy a good-quality stain and a good-quality varnish and apply them one at a time. You're going to be using those chairs and that table long after you've forgotten how much time it took to both stain and varnish all of them.

Q. I am making two leaves for an oak drop-leaf table we purchased from a dealer recently and want them to match the table as closely as possible. I found a source of quartersawn white oak, but am unsure as to how to make the leaves look as old as the table. Should any distressing be done before the finish is applied or after? What techniques do you suggest?

A. You were wise to go to whatever lengths necessary to find quartersawn white oak for your table, since it is difficult to disguise plain sawn red oak. Matching the color should only be a matter of finding the proper stain.

When distressing, or causing the wood to look older than it is, be careful not to overdo it. Distressing should be done in moderation, especially with leaves, which never receive as much abuse as the table itself. Study the table carefully and attempt to duplicate the types of wear apparent on it. Usually all that is needed is some sandpaper, a wood rasp, an awl, and a hammer or short length of chain.

The marks that are found on the table probably occurred after the finish had been applied (unless the table has been recently refinished), but many refinishers insist on distressing their work before applying a finish. I have found it best to round edges with sandpaper or a rasp before applying a finish, but I wait until after I have applied a sealer coat before adding dents with a chain or hammer.

It cannot be over stressed, however, that distressing should be done carefully and moderately and only after a good deal of study of the piece you are attempting to match.

6 / All That's Broken Is Not Lost —Making Repairs

Although stripping is messy and sanding, bleaching and staining are all time consuming, it is probably the area of repairs that keeps more people from getting very far into antique restoration. Granted, many of the necessary repairs we encounter, either in the antiques we already own or those which we are yet to buy, will have to be done in professional shops where they have specialized clamps and equipment. But that does not mean that we can't reglue a chair, fix a squeaky rocker or even redowel a broken leg in our own garage or kitchen workshop.

One of the pleasant discoveries about antique repairs is that they rarely require any specialized or expensive tools. Ninety-five percent of antique repair is strictly hand work, whether it be carving out a veneer patch with a hobby knife or splicing worn drawer runners.

Just as important as having the necessary tools is knowing when to make a repair, how to make it and how to make it last. For example:

This Eastlake-style walnut chair from the mid-Victorian period illustrates a good example of a bad repair that should be redone. The nail should be pulled, the resulting hole filled and the spot where the wood is missing patched. Note the drip of glue left by the previous refinisher. A repair such as this will only detract from the value of an antique.

Sometime early in its life someone added two diagonal cross braces to this slat-back chair, but crude as they may seem, they have become a part of the chair and should not be removed.

Q. How do you decide whether it is better to redo an earlier repair or leave it the way you found it? I have a walnut rocker dating back to the early 1800s that has many, many repairs. Some must obviously be corrected, such as nails driven through the top of the seat down into the legs, but others I'm not too sure about. For instance, someone apparently used a waxlike substance to fill a hole drilled to hold a screw or dowel attaching the arm to the back. It has shrunk and cracked, but I don't know if I should dig it out and replace it with a walnut plug. Can you give me any guidelines to follow?

A. Older, proper repairs do not necessarily detract from the overall value of an antique, but recent, improper ones can. Distinguishing one from the other, however, can lead to more disagreements than a car full of antique dealers gone "yard sale-ing."

General rules are dangerous, but the best one I can come up with is: unless you can make it stronger and look better, leave it alone. Or as someone once said, "If it ain't broke, don't fix it."

Nails, unless original, should be pulled or at least tapped in and the holes filled. Screws added later are best hidden by a plug. While we're on the subject, old plugs are generally best left alone, as are old veneer patches, old carvings and old wood replacements. As for the wax filler, so long as it is not falling out, I would leave it intact. If it is starting to break up, attempt to fill in the hole with melted lacquer or shellac sticks.

Whenever reasonably possible, later additions, such as a wooden splint or a wire wrapped around a broken spindle, should be removed and a proper repair made. The exceptions would arise in antiques so old that the repairs, even if crudely made, serve as an historical record in and of themselves.

Don't take it on yourself to have the only say in decisions that cannot easily be reversed. When in doubt, seek out the opinions of experts in the period or style of furniture you are working with. They may not all agree, but they will open your eyes to more possibilities than you might have thought existed.

Tip—Don't wait to make repairs on your damaged antiques. Pieces become lost, sharp edges get rounded and dirt prevents glue from working. The injuries won't heal themselves and can only get worse as time passes.

Q. I am having trouble getting a piece of new walnut I used to repair an old antique desk to look old. The new walnut is much darker, almost black in places, than the old, which has a nice reddish tone. Is there a secret to aging new walnut?

A. If there were, refinishers wouldn't hoard scraps of old walnut.

Naturally, whenever possible, you want to use wood as old as the antique you are repairing, but when you can't, you at least would like the patch to look inconspicuous.

First, choose a piece of wood with a grain pattern closely resembling that which it is replacing. Regardless of your staining talents, if the grain doesn't match, the repair will stand out. Second, try to select new walnut that does not have the almost black grain you described. Look, instead, for lighter walnut that will respond more readily to your needs.

Finally, there may be a secret formula some refinisher refuses to part with, but it's not here. My best results at imitating old walnut have come through a variety of cherry stains. The stain seems to give the grain the reddish hue of old walnut without darkening the wood anymore. Experiment with several different brands until you find the one that works best for your walnut.

Tip—Collect damaged and discarded table leaves as a source of old wood for your restoration projects. They are ideal for making such things as drawer fronts and commode splashboards.

Tip—If you have to replace a runner on a rocker, a chair rung, or any piece for that matter, be sure to save the old piece until after you have stained and finished the new one. It will be invaluable for exactly duplicating worn areas, unique patterns of use and other distinctive characteristics. The best restoration job is one that doesn't look like the piece has been restored.

Q. Would you explain for me the differences between the many glues on the market? I never seem to know for sure whether to use white glue, hide glue, contact cement or whatever.

A. Just as there are several strippers, stains and finishes available, each with its own strengths and weaknesses, so are there numerous adhesives for the repair of antiques. Each, too, has its own strengths and weaknesses.

The early glues were generally made from animal or fish parts and had to be heated in water before using. Animal and hide glues are still available and do form a strong bond, but are sus-

Although most home workshops won't need to stock a can or bottle of every type of glue available, different situations call for different glues. If you try to convince yourself that just one type of glue will take care of every repair you attempt, you'll end up doing many of them twice.

ceptible to both water and heat. Many traditionalists still insist on using hide glue today and consider it to be the only acceptable adhesive for true antiques.

Standard white glue is sold under a variety of brand names and is the most widely used of all the glues available. Those marked specifically for use on wood are stronger than the household, general-purpose variety. White glue is considered by most to be stronger than animal glue and more resistant to heat and water.

White glue works best on porous material and not as well on joints that have been previously glued. For best results on rungs and joints, clean all of the old glue off before applying white glue. It begins to set up after twenty minutes and, as with almost all glues, the join must be clamped for maximum results.

Epoxy is widely used in the repair of previously glued woods, but is shunned by many refinishers because they must mix the adhesive with the hardener. Epoxy works well over sealed surfaces and is better than white glue for joining two different types of material (i.e., metal to wood). It, too, must be clamped and needs twenty-four hours drying time for maximum strength.

Contact cement is primarily used for veneer repair and replacement, for no clamping is required and it works well with both porous and nonporous material. The glue is brushed onto both surfaces and allowed to dry. When the two pieces are pressed together, they adhere immediately and do not permit any additional aligning.

For the home workshop, white glue and epoxy should both be kept in stock, while contact cement can be purchased when the need arises. As previously mentioned, however, joins made with animal glue, white glue and epoxy must all be properly clamped for satisfactory results.

Tip—If your workshop area is generally unheated during the winter months, or at least very cold, keep in mind that many glues won't set up except in warm surroundings. If you can talk the rest of the family into it, the kitchen floor might be a better place to reglue your chair than a cold garage.

Q. Perhaps you can settle an argument for us. My auctioneer friend (who shall remain nameless so all his friends and customers won't realize how stupid he is) claims that he was taught to wipe the glue off immediately when you glue two pieces of wood together. I say that the glue that oozes out should be left alone and allowed to dry. Later I chip it off with a paint scraper or chisel. This way the glue stays right on top of the crack and doesn't get smeared all over like it does when you wipe it off so that the wood won't take a stain like it should. This is the way all the old woodworkers I have talked to tell me they were taught to do it. Isn't that the best way?

A. Hard as it may be to believe, your friend is right—and so are you. Before I explain, keep this in mind as you apply white glue, animal or hide glue or epoxy: a thin coat on each surface is sufficient. Any more and you just have more to wipe—or chip—off.

Which of your two methods is best depends upon the condition of the pieces of wood you are gluing together. If the wood is unfinished and will later be stained, let the glue dry untouched. Wiping it off with a rag dampened with either water or lacquer thinner will smear it across the open pores, preventing, as you mentioned, the stain from penetrating as well as it will over the rest of the wood.

Later, a sharp chisel or scraper can pop the dried glue off without gouging the wood, if you are careful. Unless you are an accomplished clamper, however, you will probably have some sanding to do anyway to get the two edges perfectly flush.

This method is unsuitable, though, for finished pieces, which you do not want to chisel or sand. If, for instance, you are gluing together two boards in a tabletop that you will not be refinishing, you will want to carefully wipe off all traces of excess glue. Water will dissolve white glue that hasn't set up and lacquer thinner will do the same for epoxy, but neither will work after the glues have dried.

Be careful when wiping off the glue not to dissolve the finish. This can happen if the old finish is susceptible to the glue solvent, as is a lacquer finish to lacquer thinner.

Check your project fifteen minutes after you have wiped off the excess glue. Often you will find traces of glue that have continued to seep out and will need to be wiped off as well.

Tip—Masking tape comes in handy for keeping glue off the wood around a repair. Run a strip down either side of a split before you clamp it and the glue will run across the tape and not your wood.

Q. I know this is going to sound stupid to all the refinishers who read your column, but I have heard you talk about epoxy and

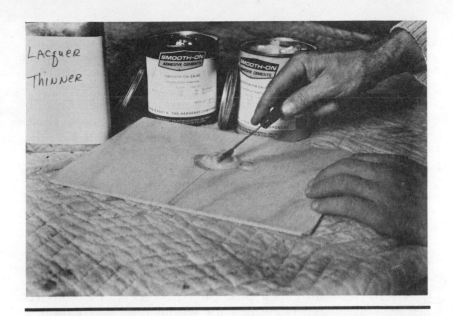

Crucial to the success of epoxy is a thorough mixing of equal parts of resin and hardener. An old putty knife makes a good spatula, while a piece of scrap wood works well as a palette.

don't know just what it is. I assume it is some type of glue, but I might be wrong about that, too. Would you mind explaining it for me?

A. Certainly not. Epoxy is a type of glue that comes in two separate tubes—one containing the resin and the other the hardener. The glue isn't activated until equal parts from the two tubes are mixed together for about thirty seconds, but then it becomes one of the strongest, toughest glues available.

Your hardware store should carry epoxy in a variety of sizes of tubes and in both the five-minute type and the regular, which takes about thirty minutes to begin to really set up. Both need to be clamped overnight, though, to achieve maximum strength.

Epoxy appears to be the best glue to use when you are joining two pieces that have been glued together once before and still have traces of old glue in their pores—and that's why you are going to hear me recommend it over and over and over again. For us refinishers it is a godsend.

Tip—Mix epoxy resin and hardener in metal jar lids (baby-food jar lids work well) to avoid having the glue drip onto either your workbench or your work. When the excess builds up, simply throw the lid away.

Tip—When using epoxy, take care not to switch the caps on the two tubes or you could find yourself in a real dilemma. There invariably is a small amount of either resin or hardener on the inside of each cap, and when they are interchanged, they become bonded to the tubes. The caps and tubes are usually well marked, but for some of us even that isn't enough to protect us from ourselves.

Tip—Drop your epoxy spatula in a can of old lacquer thinner and next time you won't have to chip off the old glue before you use it.

Q. I have just run into a problem I have never encountered before. I have been refinishing for several years and I think I follow all the suggestions from professionals like yourself.

I stripped an old walnut drop-leaf table using a good brand of paint-and-varnish remover and lacquer thinner as a rinse. One of the drop-leaves had a crack in it, so I forced epoxy (I was careful to mix equal amounts of resin and hardener) down into it and clamped it for two days.

When I took the clamps off and started sanding, the crack split open again. At first I thought maybe the wood had too much spring in it for the glue to hold, but I can easily push the two boards together with my hands. What has me worried is that the epoxy was still soft after two days and I don't think it ever really took hold. Do you have any ideas on the matter?

A. One immediately comes to mind, but only because it has happened to me before.

Undoubtedly as you were rinsing off your stripper some of your lacquer thinner seeped into the split and may have remained there even when you glued it. If so, the thinner would have interfered with the bonding action of the glue since it is also a solvent for epoxy.

Next time consider making all your glue repairs first, then strip the old finish. That way your lacquer thinner can't contaminate your repair areas. For now, however, clean out the old epoxy, let

While the traditional bar clamp at the top of the picture is a familiar fixture in most woodworking shops, the more economical pipe clamps are sufficient for home refinishing projects. It doesn't have to be pretty, it just has to work.

the split dry completely and glue it again. I think you'll find the epoxy will hold this time.

Q. The fine little carved flower petals on the back of one of my walnut chairs are coming loose and even falling off. They are too fragile to nail back on and clamping is out of the question, since they have to be positioned perfectly to look right. What is the right kind of glue to use for something like this? All I can think of is one of those super glues but I don't know if it will work on wood.

A. What you need is contact cement. Cover both the back of the carving and the spot where it is to be with a generous coat of contact cement. Let both dry for an hour and, when you bring them together, they will bond instantly.

Be careful, though, for you only get one chance. Although neither surface will stick to your finger or to dry wood, they will bond instantly and permanently to one another. You can't slide your trim around until you get it where you want it. Start by lining up one edge and then slowly press it into place. The nice thing about contact cement, though, is that just as soon as you finish you can go right on to your sanding, staining, etc.

Tip—Plastic mustard and ketchup squeeze bottles work nicely for white glue, allowing you to buy it in quarts and save money.

An assortment of C-clamps and softwood pads are a necessity for any tricky repair projects. Notice how the upholstery had to be carefully peeled back to enable the clamps to apply pressure directly over the break.

Use several, cutting the tips at different angles for pinpoint, medium and heavy flow.

Q. I have decided to invest in some clamps for my workshop. I have seen both pipe clamps and bar clamps in different workshops and was wondering which you recommended.

A. Whichever you can get the best deal on.

New bar clamps are more expensive than a new set of pipe clamps, and, although bar clamps look very professional, I don't think they justify the extra expense—nor do they have the versatility of a set of pipe clamps.

With pipe clamps you can purchase two sets of hardware and a whole pile of different-length pipes and in effect have a whole pile of clamps. When you need a 10-foot clamp to glue a couch frame you simply slide your pipe-clamp hardware on a length of 10-foot pipe and you're in business.

Tip—When removing clamps from a project, loosen them slowly, reversing the order in which they were put on. Do not

Wax paper between your antique and the clamp pad will keep excess glue from bonding the two together. Always make sure that your pads are of pine or a similar softwood or they will dent your antique.

simply remove one at a time, but release the tension on all gradually to avoid placing too much uneven stress on the new joints.

Tip—Cut up discarded softwood drawer bottoms to use as clamp pads. They won't mar the finish of your glue projects and they're cheaper than the manufactured rubber pads.

Tip—If you have difficulty juggling pipe clamps and your clamp pads, use a strip of masking tape to temporarily hold the pad in place, either on the antique or to the jaw, while you tighten the clamp.

Tip—Rather than buy expensive bar clamps for simple chair regluing, cut narrow strips from an old inner tube to form giant rubber bands. They can be twisted, tied and shortened to increase pressure and won't harm the finish on your antique.

Tip—Keep a piece of wax paper around to put between your clamp pads and your antique whenever you are regluing a joint and you won't have the problem of gluing your pad to your work.

Tip—Cut large rubber bands in half to use as clamps in gluing cracked spindles back together. Unlike C-clamps, they exert pressure from all 360 degrees simultaneously.

Tip—Use masking tape as a lightweight clamp for small, difficult-to-clamp jobs, such as splinters or wood chips. Apply pressure while anchoring the tape and make sure you don't pull your repair away when later removing the tape.

Q. I have several chairs to reglue, after many, many years of use, and am having a problem. I borrowed some pipe clamps from a neighbor, bought several tubes of epoxy as you suggested, and the chairs practically fell apart when I started to dismantle them.

Now I'm trying to glue the first one back together, but when I tighten the clamps on the legs, the clamps keep sliding until I don't have any pressure on the joints. Is there a trick to keeping clamps in place?

A. There are a few, but, depending on the angle of the legs, some might not work as well as others.

First try using triangular-shaped wedges of wood between the clamps and the chair legs. These should fool the clamp into thinking it is pulling on a right-angled leg rather than one set at 60 to 70 degrees.

If the wedges slide, tighten a C-clamp on each leg just above the wedge. Be sure to pad it as well to protect the finish. When your wedges start to inch upward, the C-clamp should stop it.

Finally, you may have to switch from pipe clamps to a belt clamp. One belt clamp can replace four pipe or bar clamps and is less apt to damage the wood. If it, too, wants to slide when you tighten it, place a board under the rungs and over the belt. Then, when the belt starts to move, the board and the rungs will hold it in place.

A belt clamp costs less than a pipe clamp but does the work of four. The board under the rungs prevents the belt from sliding up the slanted legs as pressure is applied.

Tip—White, hard-rubber mallets are the best tool for dismantling furniture; unlike the black variety, they don't leave smudge marks on the wood.

Q. We have a set of four Windsor chairs. My husband keeps gluing them together, and they keep falling apart. The biggest problem is the rungs, which refuse to stay in the legs. Is there a design problem with Windsor chairs, with the legs sticking so far out?

A. Sorry, but if there is a design problem involved, I have to side with the Windsor chair before I can side with your husband.

The legs on Windsor chairs do spread out farther than on oak pressed-back chairs, for instance, but when properly glued they will stay together just as well and for just as long. Your problem is probably either with your glue or your clamps (or lack of). Standard household glue just won't hold previously glued joints together and neither will the popular carpenter's glue. These types depend on open pores of the wood, and I'm sorry, but those just don't exist after a chair has been glued once. The best glue for old chairs is epoxy, which if we packaged and sold it as "refinisher's glue" would become a best-seller.

Tip—Avoid the expensive "dries in three to five minutes" epoxy when buying gluing supplies. An average chair will take nearly an hour to glue and you'll need the extra time to make final adjustments without breaking a fast-drying bond.

Q. I recently purchased what I think is an oak pressed-back chair. After stripping off several coats of paint, I discovered that the rungs and legs were held together with nails, but the chair is still wobbly and needs to be reglued. My husband suggested driving the nails the rest of the way in. Is this a good idea?

A. Antique collectors and refinishers spend a good deal of their spare time devising just punishments for those persons who drive nails into furniture. As you have discovered, nails seldom correct the problem, for they soon lose their strength under stress.

The best that can be said about nails is that they generally will keep the rungs and legs from actually coming apart, but they cannot match the strength of proper gluing.

It would seem that you are faced with but two alternatives.

A pair of diagonal (also called wire-cutting) pliers are an invaluable tool for removing nails from improper repairs. The softwood pad provides leverage and protects the antique from the pliers. Always wear safety glasses when pulling nails, for many times the old nails snap under pressure and can fly directly in your face.

You can leave the nails in the chair, which means you won't be able to reglue it and it will thus remain wobbly. Driving the nails deeper into the chair may tighten it temporarily, but as long as the nails are in the wood, you run the risk of the wood splitting around them any time the chair is being used.

The second alternative is much more difficult, but in the long run is the best. Using a good pair of diagonal or needle-nosed pliers, you grasp the head of the nail as best you can and pry it out.

This is easier said than done. Usually it is necessary to gouge the wood around the head of the nail to get a grip on it, and if you don't put a cloth or thin strip of wood under your pliers, the chair may soon become a mass of dents.

Be careful of two things in particular. First, you will be exerting a great deal of pressure on the tip of your pliers. Make sure that, should you slip, you won't plow a 4-inch trench across the side of your chair or the back of your hand. Second, nail heads have a way of popping off, and if you don't have eye protection, you're asking for real trouble—permanently.

After all of this and a bit of cursing, you are going to be faced with some unsightly gouges and holes. A few drops of water or the tip of an iron over a damp cloth may swell the fibers back to their normal size, but you will probably have to fall back on wood filler to make up the difference.

By the time you have finished, you most likely will have a few suggestions yourself for the person who grabs a hammer and a fistful of nails to "fix" a loose chair.

Tip—If you do much refinishing, you're going to need not just a pair of needle-nosed pliers but a pair of diagonal, or nail-cutting, pliers as well to pull all the nails you're going to find in your antiques.

Tip—Before digging out nails with your pliers, protect the wood around them with several layers of masking tape. The tape will help absorb the pressure, yet won't damage the finish when removed.

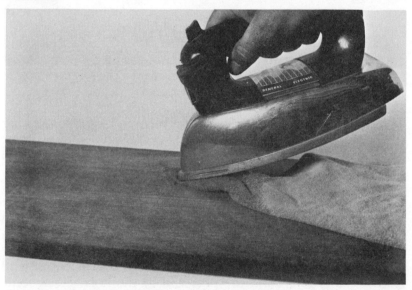

To take care of shallow dents, smuggle the iron out of the house (or your wood in). Keep the setting on Low, for the idea is to turn the water in the cloth into steam, which the wood fibers will then absorb. Don't get impatient; it may take a couple of sessions over the course of a day or so to swell the fibers back up flush with the rest of the surface. And don't burn the wood.

Q. We operate an antique shop here in Pennsylvania and each winter find that several of our chairs get very wobbly as soon as we turn the heat on. We have a humidifier, but it just can't keep enough moisture in the air to keep some of the joints from shrinking. So I spend a good deal of my winter months regluing chairs. I don't mind the ones that are practically falling apart. I just knock them apart with a rubber mallet and glue them all back together again. What I hate are the ones with only one or two loose rungs and the rest all right. The loose rungs (and sometimes just one end will be loose) won't come all the way out and it's almost impossible to get enough glue on them to work. Do you have any suggestions for gluing chairs only partially loose?

A. As you have pointed out, the key is getting glue on the end of the rung and not all over the rest of the chair. My solution came from one of my students who was a nurse and who came up with the idea of using disposable syringes and needles.

The syringes can be filled with either epoxy or white glue and the needles enable you to pinpoint where the glue is to go. Most important, they enable you to inject glue into the joints or cracks without completely dismantling the piece.

Q. Tell me, how do you solve the problem of a squeaky rocking chair? My favorite old chair has developed a bad case of squeaks, and I don't know how to get rid of them. Does this mean the chair will have to be reglued?

A. Not necessarily, though the squeaking is probably caused by the rubbing of one of the legs inside the hole in the runner. In most cases such as this, the old glue has failed and the joint is slightly loose.

If possible, determine which joint is causing the noise and force some glue around the post and in the hole. Stack some books on the seat overnight to serve as clamps while the glue dries. If you are lucky this may take care of it, but in extreme cases the chair may have to be taken apart and reglued.

P.S. If you can't get any glue in the hole, try a few drops of light oil. It won't cure the disease, but it may eliminate the symptoms.

Q. I have an oak sewing rocker that has been in my mother's family for years and is used every day. It is still in excellent condition, although the original cane has been replaced at some

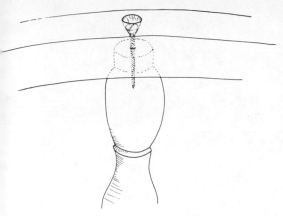

If a rocker leg refuses to stay glued in the runner, it may be necessary to drill up through the bottom of both the runner and the leg and insert a long screw. Afterwards plug the hole and sand flush.

time. Ever since I can remember it has always had a problem with the left rocker pulling away from the bottom of the leg.

It is quite annoying to feel it slip out as you rock back and then hear it pop back in when the chair comes forward again. It has been glued several times, but it looks like the hole in the rocker is just too big for the bottom of the leg. Is a small nail through the side of the rocker the best way to fix it without making a big production out of it?

A. Although the nail would probably work for a while, I don't feel it is the proper way to fix a loose runner. Several other alternatives should be considered first.

If possible, wedge slivers of wood coated with epoxy into the hole beside the leg post. Clamp firmly from the seat down to the bottom of the runner with a pipe or bar clamp and trim off any wood slivers protruding above the top of the hole.

If the stress on the front of the rocker is such that the leg still pulls out of the hole, it may be necessary to install a wood screw up through the bottom of the runner into the post. Drill a half-inch wide hole one-third of the way up into the bottom of the runner. Switch to a smaller drill bit for the pilot hole for the screw. Depending on the height of the runner, a 2- or 2½-inch screw should penetrate the leg to a point where it will hold the two together.

Q. My son recently leaned back on the legs on one of my captain's chairs and snapped off two of the five spindles in the back.

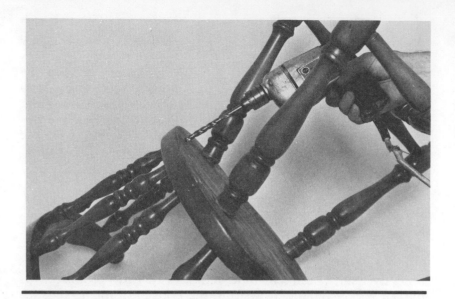

The best way to repair a broken spindle without dismantling the entire chair is to drill through the seat and through the break. A glue-coated hardwood dowel is then tapped up through the hole to bond the two pieces together.

Both broke cleanly right where the spindle goes into the seat of the chair. Can they be repaired or must they be replaced?

A. They may have to be replaced, but since that would involve some time- and/or money-consuming lathe work, try repairing them first. You've nothing to lose and everything—including some valuable experience—to gain.

Turn the chair over so that you can get an electric drill and a bit half the diameter of the spindle under the seat. While someone who trusts you holds the broken spindle in place, drill up through the bottom of the seat through the piece of spindle still in the seat and up into the bottom of the other broken piece.

Before you tap a dowel up into your fresh hole, however, move the two pieces of spindle apart and coat each jagged end with glue. Line the two up again, coat a dowel with glue and tap into place. Place a pipe clamp from the top of the chair down to beneath the seat to apply pressure to the glued joint. The combination of the dowel and the glue should keep the spindle to-

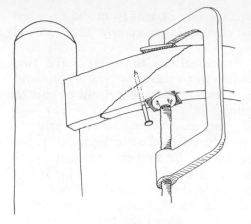

One way to keep the wood on either side of a diagonal split from sliding apart when you apply pressure with your C-clamp is to drill a hole and tap a brad up through the bottom while someone holds the two pieces in place. After the glue has dried and the clamp is removed, pull the brad and patch the hole.

gether—but you had better start chair-training your son right away.

Q. I am having a problem gluing together two pieces of wood that run at 45-degree angles to one another. Each time I attempt to clamp them, one or the other will slide up or down, depending on the angle of the pressure.

The two pieces are at the bottom of a walnut chair leg. The chair should never have been made with a splice at that particular place, since whenever someone leans back, all the weight goes right down the back legs through that joint. I have six of these chairs and all six are having the same problem.

Is there a special technique used to clamp this sort of splice, and what would you recommend doing to prevent it from splitting again?

A. Your problem is not an uncommon one, but fortunately there are a couple of possible solutions. Try any of these:

Lay your chair on its side on a wooden workbench. Set your two pieces in place, then hold them there by means of nails pounded into the workbench around the two pieces. Wedge scraps of wood between the nails and the chair to protect the finish. The nails and wedges will hold the boards in place while you clamp the joint.

Or drill a tiny hole through one of your two pieces of wood. When you have them in place, tap a brad through the hole into the other piece. The brad will keep the boards from sliding when you apply pressure with your clamps. Later, remove the brad and fill the hole.

Or, instead of using conventional C-clamps, wrap the two pieces with a length of stretched inner tube. By wraping around the ends of the joint as well as the middle, you should be able to keep the boards from slipping.

After the glue has dried, you may want to strengthen the joint—and the other joints on the chairs that haven't split yet—with a dowel through the middle of the leg perpendicular to the glue line. Drill from the inside of the leg so as to make it less noticeable and use a walnut plug to disguise the dowel (which is usually maple). If you drill carefully, you can stop just before your bit would come out the other side of the leg.

Q. I have a chair seat that I have reglued twice and it still keeps coming apart. I'm convinced that the chair wasn't designed properly, because the seat looks too wide for the support the legs are able to give it. I'm getting ready to glue and clamp it one more time before I throw it in with the yard-sale junk and let some other poor sucker buy it. Do you suggest using metal straps under the seat to keep it from splitting again?

A. I've never been a fan of metal straps on antiques or furniture, but that may be partially due to a sense of the dignity of the wood. And besides looking unsightly, the metal strap is not a guarantee that your chair won't come apart again. The problem is that it doesn't hold any weight—the screws do.

Instead of relying on just a few screws, I prefer to cut a piece of wood of the same type as the chair and both glue and screw it to the underside of the seat while it is in the clamps. Here as well as in the split in the seat itself I use epoxy.

Obviously, the thinner the piece of wood the less likely the chance it will be seen from across the room, but don't take away all its strength. Give the wood a chance and hold off on the metal strap.

Q. I have a bow-back Windsor chair that has been in our family for as long as anyone can remember. The chair has never been refinished and is still in very good condition. The only problem I am having with it is with the curved bow that holds all the spindles together. It is loose at both points where it goes through the seat.

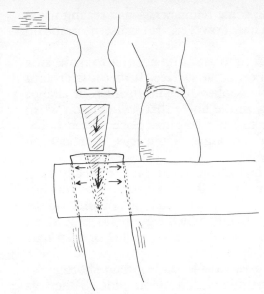

Many Windsor-style chairs have the bow held in the seat with a wedge driven up through the end of the bow. When the wedge comes loose you will need to tap it back into place with a hammer and wooden wedge of your own. This will spread the end of the bow and tighten what had been a loose back.

My husband tried to pull it out so we could reglue it, but it won't come out, yet it doesn't feel tight either. It's not nailed in, but underneath you can see that the end of the bow sticks through the bottom of the seat and looks like it is split. Is there anything we can do to tighten it?

A. Many of the bows of Windsor and Windsor-style chairs were held in place with a wedge driven up into each end. The bow was first notched, then drawn into place. When the wedge was driven up into the wood, the bow would swell and fit snugly.

I would suggest tapping the wedge in your chair gently with a hammer and a small piece of wood shaped to cover just the head of the wedge. By driving the wedge in just a fraction of an inch, you can eliminate any looseness.

If the wedge is missing, as it often is, cut a new one from a piece of maple or birch and tap into place.

Q. I have so many chairs coming apart that I decided to invest in my own set of pipe clamps so I could reglue them and save some money. I thought the first one went real well; it came right apart, I cleaned off the old glue, used epoxy, and clamped it all together. The next day when I took off the clamps, the chair didn't sit level and now my wife won't let me touch another one until I fix this one.

A. Most people—including some refinishers—just reach for the saw when that happens. That, however, can cause more problems than it solves.

The best way to keep it from happening again is to make sure you are gluing your chairs on a flat surface. If that wasn't your problem, then you probably applied pressure from your clamps unevenly. Watch the marks in the finish that will tell you when the rungs are pulled back to their original place in the holes. Overclamping may distort the angle of the legs, thus causing your chair to sit unevenly.

Finally, to repair your first chair, set it on a perfectly level surface, such as a table saw. We will assume that since you just glued it, taking it apart will prove difficult, if not impossible, without extensive damage. Identify which legs are now too short or too long. If the problem is minor, a wood file or rasp may solve it.

If the difference is too great to file, rather than shorten the long leg, lengthen the short one with a nylon glide. If the legs already have glides, remove the one on the longest leg. Either way, you should be able to get permission to glue the remainder of your chairs.

Tip—Don't get in a hurry to cut down table or chair legs that aren't all even. Besides creating a larger problem than you had before, you may find that what sits level in one part of your home doesn't in another. Instead, tap nylon leveling caps onto the short legs. Later, the caps can be taken off if necessary, but it is difficult to reverse the sawing process. As one of my ex-employees once complained, "I sawed it twice and it's still too short, boss."

Q. I have a problem and I also think I have a solution—sort of. I have a table with a broken leg. I read an article several months ago where the author described a process of gluing the break together and then—and I think I'm right—cutting the same leg in two above the break so a dowel could be put down through the break.

Have you heard of such a repair or do I have it all wrong?

A. Yes, I've certainly heard of it, and no, you don't have it all wrong.

When a break is jagged or uneven it can be difficult to deter-

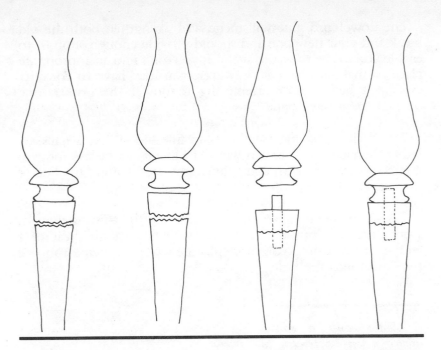

Drastic as it may seem, sometimes the best way to repair a jagged break involves cutting the leg in two nearby. The original break can then be glued and, later, a dowel inserted through it and the cut for additional support.

mine the exact center of each piece to drill for a dowel. Obviously, finding the exact center is crucial or the two pieces won't line up when brought together with the dowel in place.

I have in the past actually cut the leg in two above or below the break *if* there was a turning nearby that would disguise the new cut. The ideal situation occurs in spool turnings, where you can make a thin hacksaw-blade cut in the valley of one of the turnings where no one will notice.

If you can disguise a new cut nearby, cut the leg in half, glue the old break together, then wait twenty-four hours. The glue will hold the old break together while you drill through the new cut up (or down) through the old break. Glue in a dowel, letting it protrude out of the new cut so you can drill and dowel it at the same time (see illustration above).

The dowel and glue will mend and strengthen both the old break and your new one and should provide enough support to enable you to use the table again. If you can't find an appropriate place to make a new cut, however, you may have to consider making a new leg or attempting to dowel the broken one through the jagged ends.

Tip—When making small cuts in fine wood, use a hacksaw rather than a traditional handsaw. The fine teeth are less apt than even a backsaw to chip and splinter the wood along the line of the cut.

Tip—When making repairs with glue and tight-fitting dowels, score a groove along the dowel to let the trapped air ahead of it escape. If you don't, you may split the wood by trying to force the dowel into the hole.

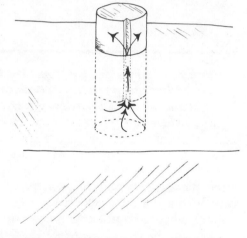

A dowel with a scored groove down its length to vent off trapped, compressed air and extra glue.

Q. We recently purchased a 42-inch square oak table with five large legs from a local dealer. The table had been stripped by a refinisher with a dip tank, but had not been refinished.

We are in the process of finishing the table ourselves, but since this is the first project of any size for us, we have a few questions. First the legs. As I said, they are quite large—nearly 6 inches in diameter—and very decorative. Each leg was made by gluing several boards together and now it looks as if some of them are coming apart.

In several places there is a gap nearly ⅛ of an inch wide and several inches long. Should these be glued and clamped together or filled with some sort of wood putty? My husband thinks the dipping caused the legs to come apart. If so, will they continue to separate?

A. It certainly is not unusual for the large, almost bulbous, legs of the late Victorian square oak tables to begin to separate after eighty to one hundred years' use. As you pointed out, the legs were almost always composed of several boards glued together before being put on the lathe.

I don't think it would be fair to assume that dipping was solely responsible for the separation of the boards. It is not unheard of for the outside boards on large legs to warp slightly and break the glue bond, especially when you consider the susceptibility of the old glues to both heat and moisture. Once the separation started, any substance harmful to the old glue, such as stripper or water, would have been able to penetrate and dissolve even more glue.

In many such situations, clamping has caused more damage than it averted. If an outside board on a leg is warped slightly, forcing it back into place may only result in it splitting. Disguising the gap between the boards can be accomplished using standard wood dough, which, when dry, can be sanded, stained and finished, or by gluing in thin strips of oak. Personally, I prefer the latter, for wood dough has a tendency to split and crumble when used to cover large or flexible areas.

If you do need to glue sections back together, clean off all traces of old glue and coat both surfaces with a thin layer of epoxy. In place of bar or pipe clamps, wrap the two pieces with stretched strips of tire inner tubes. Make sure that you place a piece of wax paper between the glue joint and the giant rubber bands to keep from gluing them to the legs.

Q. We recently moved to this area, and while we were rearranging the furniture in our home, our square oak table fell apart. What happened is that we had to turn it on its side to get it through a doorway, and when we did, the screws that hold the extenders on pulled out.

My husband tried breaking off wooden match sticks and gluing them in the holes, but the screws still pulled out. Do we need to go to larger screws or is there another way to remedy the situation? Right now we are eating off a card table while our oak table leans against the wall.

A. There is another way to repair your table—but don't put the card table away just yet.

You will need to clear a section of your carpet so you can turn the table on its back and leave it there for at least a day. I would suggest you pick a time when you aren't hosting the women's club or a pack of cub scouts.

Dig or drill out the match sticks and old glue and get a section of hard-maple dowel that will completely fill the hole. Cut the dowel into short lengths, coat either the inside of the hole or the ends of the dowel lengths with epoxy glue and then tap them into the holes (see illustration below).

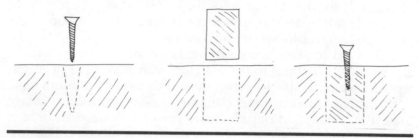

When a screw hole is worn to the point where it will no longer hold the threads of the screw, you may need to drill it out with a ½-inch drill, glue in a hard-maple dowel and redrill your hole after the glue has dried.

Let the glue dry for a day, then trim off any dowel sticking above the surface of the wood. Redrill the screw holes with the proper size drill bit and align your extenders over them.

Don't make the mistake of switching to a larger screw that also turns out to be longer. If you do, you may end up screwing your table to the floor—and that can be awkward to explain to your guests.

• • •

Old screws always seem to cause problems. If they're not broken in half, they're rusted in place. If they're not rusted in place, they're just plain missing. No questions on this topic, but we did get a few tips from our readers:

Tip—Keep a broken hacksaw blade on hand to cut fresh slots on worn or broken screw heads. Wrap electrical tape around one end of the blade to form a handle.

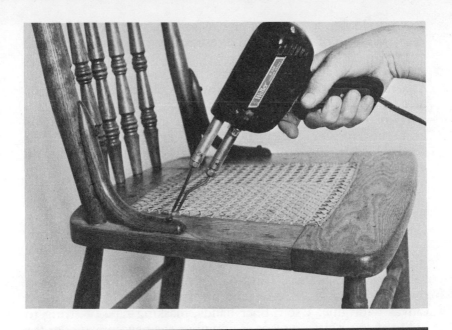

One way to convince a stubborn screw to come out without ruining either the slot or your chair is to heat the head of it with a soldering gun. Give it a few minutes to cool, during which time the expansion and contraction of the metal will loosen the grip of the threads on the wood.

Tip—To help facilitate the removal of stubborn screws, place your screwdriver in the slot, then tap the end of it with a hammer. The vibrations will break the threads loose from the fibers of the wood and enable you to back the screw out easily.

Tip—Old woodworkers kept a chunk of beeswax handy to rub across the threads of screws before inserting them. Paste wax works as well, but soap can cause them to rust and resist ever coming out again.

Q. We are in the process of restoring a Hoosier kitchen cabinet, but don't know how to fix the roll. The slats are still in place, but the canvas holding them together is split in several spots. As a result, the slats jam easily and the canvas continues to tear when we try to loosen it. Can you give us some advice on repairing it? We've done all of the rest of the restoration ourselves and would like to do this as well.

A. Great—and there's no reason why you should have to stop here.

To make the repair you will need to remove the entire roll from the Hoosier. It may be a bit tricky to get back in once repaired, so be sure to remember exactly how it came out. You may even need to spread the sides of the cabinet a half inch or more both to take the roll out and put it in later.

Lay the roll out on a work surface with the canvas side up. Begin by gluing down any loose pieces of old canvas to the slats. Cover with wax paper and weight. Find a well-stocked fabric store that carries lightweight waterproof canvas and get a piece slightly larger than your roll.

Cut your new canvas 1 inch larger than the original and, after the first glue has dried, coat both the new and the back of the old canvas with glue. Use rubber bands, masking tape or string to hold any loose slats in place as you press the new canvas over the old. Smooth out air bubbles and excess glue with a small block of wood, then cover the entire area with wax paper. Stack on the paper any available weights—boards, books, bricks, etc. After the glue has dried, trim off the excess fabric and glue, and re-install the roll.

Q. I am refinishing an old family china cupboard made of walnut. Both the lower doors and the sides have ¼-inch thick panels in them. The boards that make the frames around these panels were coming apart so I finished dismantling them so I can reglue them. My question is this: when I reglue the doors should I glue the panels in the slots for extra strength?

A. No. Even though they may have been glued in previously, these panels were meant to "float" in the grooves surrounding them. That way they could expand and contract with the change in seasons without splitting or buckling.

Q. I have an old walnut dresser, with two handkerchief drawers on the top and a splashboard, that was given to me by my grand-mother several years ago. The finish is still good, but the three lower drawers no longer work well. A friend suggested that I wax the runners, but when I took the drawers out I could see that the runners on the bottom of each of the drawers had almost completely worn away. One is so bad that the bottom of the drawer has a groove worn in it. What I don't know is if I'll have to have someone make new drawers using the old fronts or if the old ones can be repaired.

A. Worn drawer slides can be fixed, although if they are really bad—as yours may well be—it can be a tedious task. If you don't fix them, though, eventually the bottom of the drawer will wear through and you'll have to replace it, too.

Turn a drawer upside down and, with a sharp knife or chisel, cut away any useless slivers and square off the bottoms of the worn runners. Cut a piece of hardwood to build each runner back up to its original height (see illustration below). Coat both surfaces with white glue and clamp in place. After the glue has dried, sand the outside of the new wood flush with the side of the drawer and stain to match. Later, seal all exposed new wood with sanding sealer, varnish or shellac. Finally, wax if necessary.

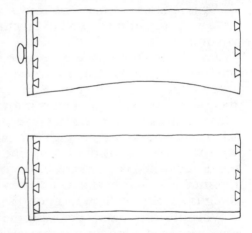

Softwood drawer runners wear out after a number of years and will need to be built back up to their original level. First trim away enough wood from the runner to give your new piece a flat surface to join, then glue and clamp. The next day sand and stain to blend in with the original.

Q. I do a lot of my own refinishing and seem to encounter a lot of drawer bottoms that need to be replaced in desks and dressers. Most of them have a real thin board in them, but I have found it too expensive to have a cabinet shop plane down a ¾-inch thick board to ¼ inch just for a drawer bottom. Masonite doesn't look right and neither does plywood. What do you use for drawer bottoms and where do you get it?

A. On true antiques—those museum-quality pieces that deserve perfect restoration—I go to the extra expense of finding a board of the same type as that which has to be replaced and having it planed down to the necessary thickness. (I won't, however, replace the original if there is any way it can be saved and repaired.)

On our more common "antiques"—that to a museum would be just old furniture—I have found that oak-, birch- or walnut-veneered plywood works best for drawer bottoms. Lumber yards won't always carry it in ¼ inch thicknesses, so check with local cabinet shops. They use it all the time.

Q. I have a walnut commode that has been in our family for several years. My daughter took it with her to school for her apartment last fall, but when she brought it back the top had warped.

There are several black rings on it as well, which leads me to believe she had plants sitting on it. I suppose the water could have made the top warp. Do you have any suggestions on getting it flat again?

A. Some boards can never be convinced to flatten out once they have warped, but there is an old method that you should at least attempt.

Remove the top of the commode by taking out the series of screws holding it on from underneath. Strip off the old finish and sand lightly. To get rid of the warp, wet the concave side and lay the top, convex side up, on a wet towel spread out on concrete. This will work indoors, but if you can do it outside it works even faster. Place some weights such as bricks or plastic milk jugs filled with sand on top of the warp. The idea is rather simple: the underside will take in moisture, the upper side will release moisture and the weights will flatten the warp out when everything is equal (see illustration on facing page.)

When the top is flat, take it off the wet towel, lay it on a flat, dry surface and, with the weights back on it again, let it dry. Get right to your refinishing the next day, however, and be sure to finish both sides to keep it from warping again.

Q. We have been given an old wooden swinging cradle that has ends of bentwood and spindles. One of the bentwood ends has worn through at the top and has some splits in it where it curves. Would you know where we can get this piece replaced, or is there a way to repair it? We have all the spindles and the broken piece. It would be lovely if we can only find a way to repair it.

A. You need to concentrate your efforts on either repairing or having the broken piece repaired rather than replaced. Having a new piece steamed and bent would be expensive and would detract from the looks and value of the cradle.

Splits in the curved portion can be glued down and held in place with masking tape or small C-clamps while the glue dries. The break in the bow will be more difficult, but hopefully a splice can be inserted underneath to bond the two pieces. Glue or clamp the two pieces together and then carve out a slot on the underside into which you can glue a strip of hardwood (see illustration on page 144).

Plastic milk jugs filled with sand make excellent weights for pressing the warp out of a board. Place the piece of wood on a wet towel with the convex side up and two or three weights on it. As the bottom side absorbs moisture, the weights will force the hump back down into place.

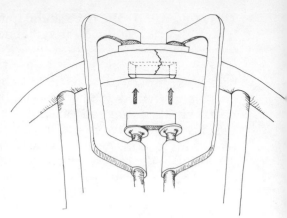

A wood splice is clamped into and across the break in the bow, then sanded flush later. Even though no one should even know it's there when you are finished, make sure the splice is the same type of wood as the bow.

After the glue has hardened, sand the splice flush with the bow. The repair may not be 100 percent as strong as the original, so inform everyone in the family that the cradle is not to be picked up or moved by grabbing at that point.

Tip—Invest in a small box of single-edged razor blades for your refinishing work area. They are unsurpassed for trimming veneer, pressed cane and masking tape and work beautifully for taking paint off mirrors and glass. *Note:* they also cut flesh very easily, as my fingers will attest, so be careful—or buy one of those inexpensive holders.

Tip—For the accident-prone refinisher: bloodstains can be removed from wood with a rag dampened with common hydrogen peroxide.

• • •

We certainly can't end our chapter on repairs with a tip like that. Bloodstains? Certainly not ours, I hope. Repairs can be the most challenging aspect of antique restoration and don't have to become the most frustrating. Think through carefully everything you do and remember—treat each piece with the respect it deserves. Properly treated, a good antique can outlive several owners—just so long as there are one or two good restorers around.

7 / The Finishing Touch

I f you include everything from factory lacquers to homemade concoctions of shoe polish and tung oil, we must have over a dozen different finishes to choose from for our antiques. Picking one—the right one—can be even more confusing than picking a good stripper, deciding whether to use wood dough, wood putty or wood in a repair, or selecting a stain. Fortunately, many finishes can be eliminated for obvious defects or because they have been surpassed by yet another finish. A good example of that would be shellac, which more than one of our readers have asked about:

Q. Years ago my mother finished all of her wooden furniture with shellac. Is this still considered a good finish?

A. If used within strict guidelines, shellac is still a good finish, but modern technology has improved varnish and lacquer to the point where it has become impractical to revert to shellac.

— 145 —

Shellac's two greatest advantages, namely that it dries quickly and can be touched up easily, are offset by the fact that it has little resistance to either water or heat and virtually none to alcohol. A spilt drink, an overwatered plant or a steaming bowl of soup can all leave their mark on a shellac surface. Items such as picture frames and mantle clocks lend themselves well to being shellacked, but tables, chairs, chests and other pieces that make heavy demands on a finish will need more protection.

Tip—If you use shellac because it dries quickly and thus makes a good sealer under your varnish, be sure to check the date on the lid. If the shellac is more than a year old, don't use it.

. . .

Before getting too far into a discussion of the advantages and disadvantages of the different finishes we have to choose from, though, we need to talk about the one thing all finishes have in common: the need for a proper work place in which to apply them. Even if, as in the case of lacquer, it needs only a few minutes to set up, every finish has to have time to dry in a relatively dust-free environment. If those conditions do not exist and you are using a finish with a slow drying time, such as varnish, then you might end up writing a letter that sounds like this:

Q. After I finished varnishing the top of my round oak table the surface feels rough and bumpy. What did I do wrong?

A. Where do I start?

A rough finished surface can be the result of any of the following: applying varnish over an improperly prepared surface, brushing on your finish without first getting all of the dust out of the pores, shaking rather than stirring the varnish, using a dirty brush or working in a high-traffic area.

In any event, either dust particles or air bubbles have dried in your varnish. Our number-one suspect is the place where you work, for since varnish takes around four hours to dry to the touch, the combination of dust in the air and any unnecessary movement in the room will result in a virtual avalanche of particles tumbling down into your wet, sticky surface. There they will dry and harden, leaving you with a tabletop that looks and feels much like a piece of coarse sandpaper.

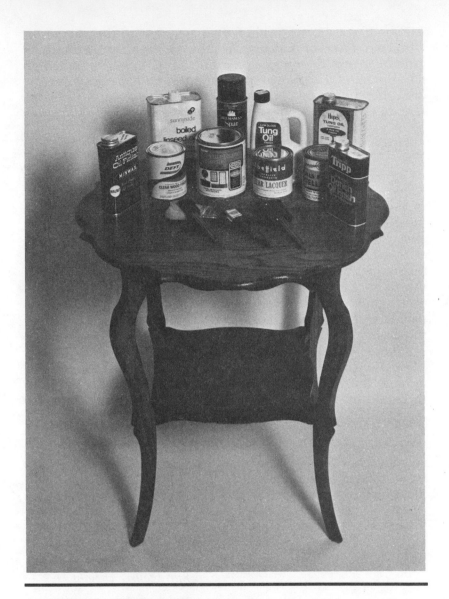

The secret to choosing the best finish for your project is not trying to find just one for all your projects. Each type of finish available has its strengths and weaknesses. And buy small—it is better to buy a pint now and another pint two months from now than to buy a quart and risk it becoming contaminated in the meantime.

Tip—If you have no other alternative but to do your restoration work near or under an air vent, use duct tape to attach an extra filter over the outside of the opening. It will cut down on the amount of dust blown over your projects and save you some difficult rubbing out. Better yet, before you varnish, turn the furnace down or the air conditioner off until the finish dries.

. . .

Tips, tips and more tips.

Tip—Don't forget—or try to forget—to use a tack rag before varnishing. It can pick up microscopic bits of dust that, a few minutes later, would have been bobbing along behind your brush. You don't have to buy tack rags, however, for you can save yourself some money by making your own. Dampen a piece of cheesecloth with a couple of tablespoons each of varnish and turpentine, working the two into the cloth, then wringing out the excess. Let dry slightly until the rag becomes tacky, but store in a tightly closed container to keep it from drying out completely. If it does dry out, simply work in another tablespoon of turpentine.

Tip—Even new brushes can contain dirt or dust. Before varnishing, dip your brush in mineral spirits, then shake out both the liquid and the dirt. Dry with a clean, lint-free cloth and go to it.

Tip—Always apply your finish with the work surface between you and your primary source of light. This way you'll spot dry areas, cat hairs and brickbats before your varnish dries. And those brickbats are tough to sand out.

Keep your work surface between you and your primary source of light.

Tip—If you are bothered by stain, varnish or shellac building up around the top of the can and then running down the side when you tap the lid back on, take an awl and punch several holes in the bottom of the groove. The liquid will then run back down into the can and not down the outside.

To prevent varnish from running down the side of the can, punch holes in the channel around the can's top.

Tip—Several 2-foot lengths of electrical wire hung from the ceiling in your work area come in handy for hanging parts, such as table legs and spindles, while they dry. If necessary, tap a small nail in the end of the leg or spindle where it won't show to hook the wire to.

Tip—This suggestion came from a reader in West Branch, Iowa, just before press time so I haven't had an opportunity yet to try it out, but it sounds as if it should work. She asserts that if you need to store your used brushes temporarily between coats, your freezer will prevent them from drying up. Wrap them in wax paper and, she adds, don't forget to label them. Not only will that avoid some confusion, but it could keep your family from thinking you've got a new kind of frozen dinner for them—"filet de vernis."

. . .

Now that we've got an idea what is required in terms of a work environment, we can get down to business. As I said before, we have many, many different finishes to choose from, but we won't be able to adequately discuss each one here. Varnish, lacquer, shellac, boiled linseed oil and tung oil are a few of the more well known and have generated the most letters, so those are the ones we will concentrate on.

First, though, there is the problem of a sealer. Many stains claim to both stain and seal the surface of the wood, which is true in one respect. Sanding sealer, however, is generally considered to be a thin finish that is applied, allowed to dry and then sanded to provide the final coat of varnish (does not apply to oil finishes) with a smooth surface. And as we all know—the smoother the surface, the smoother the finish. Consider:

Q. Several books I have picked up on refinishing talk about using a sanding sealer after staining but before varnishing. I have always used tung oil, but since I am doing a square oak table I wanted to use a varnish for more protection. Is a sanding sealer really necessary?

A. Sealers require an extra step in the restoration process and a few extra materials, but are well worth the effort. They hold the stain and filler in the wood and prevent both from floating up into the finish. They also resist moisture and heat, thus giving the wood added protection from abuse. In addition, they prevent the final finish from soaking too far into the wood, leaving unsightly dry spots that necessitate an additional coat.

Perhaps most important, though, is the effect sealers have on the feel of the finish. When properly rubbed out with #220 sandpaper or #000 steel wool, they provide a smooth surface for your final finish. As a result, your varnish will flow smoothly across the wood and will need less rubbing out to achieve a professional-looking appearance.

Make sure that your sealer is compatible with your intended finish by reading the directions on your can of finish. If you do not wish to purchase commercially prepared sanding sealer, an all-purpose sealer can be made by combining three parts denatured alcohol with one part shellac. It dries quickly, is highly compatible with nearly every type of finish and sands easily.

Tip—Apply sealer to all parts of the piece you are refinishing, including the underside of tables and chairs, drawer sides and bottoms and the backs of dressers and chests. Bare wood needs to be sealed to protect it against dirt, moisture and abuse; the sealer will also help prevent damage caused by warping during wet seasons and splitting during dry.

• • •

Of all the finishes available, standard varnish has been the most popular over the years. Though its standing is now being threatened both by tung oil and by its first cousin, polyurethane varnish, it is still the most dependable finish you can use. Like all finishes, though, it has its drawbacks, but most of them come in the application stage and not in the amount of protection it gives or the effect it has on the appearance of the antique.

All wood needs to have a finish or it will swell during times of high humidity and crack when the air is dry. Coat the undersides of chairs with sanding sealer, shellac, thinned varnish, tung oil or just about any finish you have around. It's a perfect way to use up an old can of finish that you wouldn't trust anywhere else.

Q. It seems that years ago all anyone ever used for varnishing was a special and expensive pure-bristle varnish brush. A few years ago disposable foam brushes were the rage. Now it seems that everyone I talk to who refinishes furniture tells me they put their varnish on with a rag.

I'm still using my varnish brush, but now I'm wondering if I shouldn't switch to one of these newer methods. Do you recommend one over the others?

A. All three, the bristle brush, the foam brush and the rag method, have their good and bad points, and I would no more recommend just one than I would discard all three.

The traditional bristle brush is the most expensive to buy and the most tedious to properly care for, but in return will lay on a smooth, even coat of varnish without a struggle. The foam brush is inexpensive and requires no upkeep since it is thrown away afterwards. It too works nicely with varnish and is excellent for brushing straight lines or edges. It doesn't hold up well under hard or prolonged use, however, and does not work as well as the bristle brush for "tipping off" (the final step in varnishing where the brush in one movement is lightly stroked across the varnished area to smooth out the varnish).

The rag method would appear to be the cheapest of the three, but you must make sure that your choice of rags is limited to lint-free material. It works well on small articles for which you don't want to dirty your bristle brush or waste a foam one. The rag method, however, runs into problems on intricate carvings or moldings, for it is difficult to get into crevices without risking runs. Tipping off is out of the question, for with a rag you can create more lines than you erase.

Tip—To avoid lap marks when brushing on stain, shellac, varnish or paint, start each new brushful a few inches this side of where you left off. After you have brushed out the majority of the liquid in your bristles, go back and tie in the space between your last brushful and the current one.

Tip—Here is a fourth option for applying varnish: rather than buy an expensive varnish brush and try to clean it thoroughly after each use, start each varnish project with a new, inexpensive synthetic bristle brush that you will use the next time only for staining or stripping. It's a small price to pay to keep your varnish jobs dirt free.

Tip—Keep a spare dry brush handy while you are varnishing to pick up excess varnish in carvings, grooves and turnings before it dries. Works as well for taking out runs and sags.

Q. I'm having a problem with the urethane varnish I'm putting on an oak tabletop. I like an oil finish, but with two small children I have to have all the protection I can get, so that's why I'm using polyurethane.

The problem is that I'm getting brush marks dried in the finish. I brush on the varnish directly from the can, then to smooth it out, dip a rag in mineral spirits and wipe over it gently. The next day, though, the marks are still there. What should I do?

A. Throw that d%&#@%)+* rag away!

The more you mess with varnish, the more mess you make. Stir it thoroughly, pour a portion of the varnish into a clean jar and thin it down with a little mineral spirits (one blop per pint) to help it flow out. Take a clean brush and work the varnish into the pores as you brush it on. Then "tip off" by running the tip of your brush (*not* a rag) the length of each board, with the grain. Then leave it alone. Don't go back over it, don't dab at it, don't touch it, don't even look at it. Lock yourself in a closet if you have to, but don't mess with it.

Tip—Never shake a can of varnish, because if you do, you'll create hundreds of tiny air bubbles that your brush will transfer onto the wood. There they will harden and leave you with a tabletop resembling a lunar surface. For best results always stir varnish with a clean stirring stick in a figure-eight pattern.

Always stir your varnish in a figure-eight pattern. Shaking it will create thousands of bubbles—and a finish resembling a piece of your grandmother's peanut brittle.

Q. I seem to have problems with my varnish not drying within the twenty-four hours specified on the can. Would placing freshly varnished pieces in the sun on a nice day speed the process?

A. Either varnishing outdoors or taking a freshly varnished piece of furniture outside is asking for trouble. Even if kids, cats, dogs and nosy neighbors (the kind who wipe a finger across the top and *then* ask "Is it dry yet?") could be kept under control, the dust in the air cannot. In addition, you won't fully appreciate the vast number of tiny insects inhabiting the air space above your yard until you provide them with a wet, sticky surface for a landing pad.

The heat from the sun would probably speed up the drying process, but it would cause problems as well. Varnish dries slowly, but for a reason. The finish is less brittle than fast-drying lacquer and thus withstands more abuse without chipping. Part of this is due to the curing process that takes place as the varnish hardens to the touch. Even after it appears to be dry, the finish will continue to cure and harden. If a second coat is put on too soon, the curing process is interrupted, leaving you with a thick, soft finish.

Tip—Those of you who are discovering in the midst of a humid summer that varnish can seem to take forever to dry might want to consider adding a little japan drier to each quart of finish. Contrary to what you might think, thinning varnish actually slows down the drying process, so you may want to use japan drier all the time if you are in the habit of thinning your varnish to make it flow better.

Q. What can I do about the tiny bumps I always get in my finish after I varnish?

A. Those tiny little bumps are particles of dust, and if they're not coming from your brush or up out of the pores of the wood, then they're dropping down out of the air.

Since there is no practical way you can completely avoid dust in the air, the final solution to your problem comes after the varnish has dried. After your first coat has hardened (no less than twenty-four hours later), buff the surface with dry #000 steel wool. Repeat this after the final coat, but with #0000 steel wool moistened with lemon oil.

In extreme cases, such as when your son turns the thermostat up and the furnace kicks in, spewing dust out of the vent and over the top of your table, you will have to gently sand the top with #400 or finer wet/dry sandpaper dipped in water. This technique is called "wet sanding" and is used a great deal by auto body shops, whose techniques and materials are light-years ahead of wood refinishers'. Afterwards, have your son buff the finish with the steel wool and lemon oil.

Q. I have been interested in antiques for several years, but not until recently have I had either the time or the space to refinish any of the things I have bought. I have been attending several local auctions and have begun buying oak pieces in need of refinishing. I am confused, though, about the difference between polyurethane varnishes and regular varnish. At an auction last week I overheard two men talking about how terrible it was that so many of the antiques there had been refinished with polyurethane, but friends of mine have refinished almost all their antiques using nothing else. Could you explain the difference between the two and recommend one?

A. Polyurethane, Varathane, urethane and similar sounding varnishes are a rather recent addition to the line of refinishing products, but have become popular so quickly that many stores no longer carry standard varnish.

The urethane varnishes contain a plastic additive (or similar material) that offers wood more protection against harsh treatment than the same number of coats of any other finish. Originally it was intended for bar tops, for it was designed to withstand excessive amounts of water, alcohol, heat and abuse.

Many professional collectors, dealers and restorers, however, avoid urethane varnishes for several reasons. First, since urethane finishes are a rather recent invention, using them runs counter to the philosophy that true restoration work should seek to restore an antique to its original condition and not to modernize it.

Second, urethane finishes have a tendency to look and feel "slick." They almost always are glossier than standard varnish finishes and often appear thick, more as if they had been poured onto the wood rather than soaking into and becoming a part of the antique. Finally, since they do contain plastic or plasticlike additives, urethane varnishes do not respond well to the final rubbing out. Thus it is difficult to obtain the highly desirable satin-smooth finish produced by craftsmen for centuries.

Traditional varnish is to some more difficult to apply, for to obtain protection similar to that offered by urethane finishes, one coat of sanding sealer and two coats of varnish should be brushed on. Even this may not surpass the protection of plastic, but very few antiques ever require the defenses designed for bars. Rubbed out with #0000 steel wool, #400 sandpaper or pumice and rottenstone and topped with a coat of paste wax, traditional varnish will provide a water, heat and alcohol resistant finish without the look and feel of plastic.

A recommendation? Choose the finish that best suits the piece.

Q. I am refinishing a walnut five-legged drop-leaf table for some friends of mine. They insist that I use a urethane-type finish on the top because they have small children and want to be able to use the table for their meals each day. I tried to explain that regular varnish would look more natural on the table, which, by the way, is a fine-looking antique, but they want nothing other than urethane varnish.

My problem is that I can't seem to avoid having the finish look streaky. After the first coat, I thought the streaks would disappear when it dried; then I thought they would go away if I put another coat on. Instead, the table looked worse. I was so embarrassed I stripped off the two coats before anybody saw it. What can I do now to keep it from streaking again?

A. One of the unfortunate drawbacks of urethane varnishes is that they do tend to streak, although the streakiness can be reduced to what we hope is an acceptable level.

Most manufacturers do not recommend it, but I thin urethane varnishes slightly, whenever I use them, with a little bit of turpentine or mineral spirits. I'm not sure if it will reduce streaking, but I have found that the disposable foam brushes eliminate almost all brush strokes and certainly all bristles from the finish. Hopefully either of these techniques will help reduce a good deal of the streakiness, but so long as there is a plasticlike additive in the varnish, the tendency to streak is going to be there as well.

Q. We are refinishing an old oak door for the front of our new home. We have stripped and sanded it and are getting ready to put on a finish, but don't know exactly what kind would be best. Several different people have recommended several different brands and kinds, but we just don't know what to use. Could you suggest something?

A. Several different finishes might work, but I have had the best experiences with exterior spar varnish. I never use it on furniture, even if the manufacturer recommends it, but I keep it on hand just for doors like yours.

Q. Is tung oil considered a good finish?

A. Homer Fornby (of Fornby refinishing products) thinks so, but some might think he is a bit prejudiced. Life would be so much easier if there were but one finish to suit all of our refinishing needs, but it just isn't so. Tung oil, like all finishes, has its strengths and its weaknesses, its advantages and its disadvantages.

Like any oil finish, tung oil is light bodied and is rubbed into the wood with either a soft cloth or with your hand (personally, I prefer a cloth). The next day the piece should be rubbed with a clean dry cloth and the next coat applied. Unlike some oil finishes, tung oil does not harden as it sinks into the wood. It is water resistant, although coat for coat it does not offer the protection of either varnish or lacquer. For it to be truly effective, then, several coats must be applied. I think the old rule for linseed-oil finishes applies as well to tung oil: once a day for a week, once a week for a month, once a month for a year and once a year forever.

One of the most attractive aspects of tung oil is its ease of application; all you need is a soft, clean rag. The problem is that you need it several times—at least a half dozen or so—before the tung oil begins to build up on the surface of the wood.

Tung oil is at its best on tight-grained woods such as hard maple, walnut and any type of burl veneer. Oak presents a problem, for the oil has little surface build-up ability and has trouble ever filling the pores completely. On the proper piece and with diligent application, though, a tung-oil finish is unsurpassed for enhancing the natural beauty of a true antique.

Tip—Heat your tung oil slightly before applying and it will spread more easily. Remove the cap and set the can in a pan of hot water for a few minutes to warm the liquid.

Q. I know you get a lot of questions about tung oil, but I don't think I've seen anything about my problem. I refinished a walnut dining room style chair that has a caned seat. The chair has curved hip rests, a nice piece of burl walnut across the back slat and it dates back to the late 1800s. I rubbed in six coats of tung oil and am really happy with the way each coat built up on the one before it, but each time the finish got glossier and glossier. I want more of a satin look, not high gloss. Do you have any ideas? I didn't use low-gloss tung oil because I thought it would be too flat. If I have to, I'll strip the chair again and start over.

A. By all means, don't undo what you've already done so well. Take a pad of #0000 steel wool (nothing else) and begin lightly rubbing down your chair. Don't give it a high-speed buffing. By gently rubbing the steel wool over the dried tung oil you can gradually reduce the gloss to the exact point where it pleases you. Afterwards, wipe the piece clean with a soft, dry cloth and save all that stripping energy for your next project.

Q. Have you ever heard of mixing turpentine and tung oil together as a finish? Well, my husband has, and I made the mistake of listening to him and now I have a real mess on my hands.

He swears that a refinisher he knows mixes tung oil and turpentine together and then slops it on the wood he's refinishing, especially walnut, and lets it sit and soak in. Last night I followed his directions and this morning I found the worst mess I have ever seen in several years of refinishing my own antiques.

This concoction dried into a sticky, gooey mess that smears when I try to wipe it up and just looks horrible. I don't think it has ruined the wood underneath, but what do I use to try to clean up this mess? I'm thinking of giving it to my husband and sending them both to his refinisher friend.

A. It sounds to me like there was a key bit of information left out somewhere between the refinisher friend and your husband's instructions. Mixing turpentine and tung oil together is safe enough, but the problem came in when the time element was left to chance.

Rather than letting the mixture sit overnight, you should have wiped it off about twenty minutes later. What happens is that the varnish in the tung oil soon begins to set up, and if you leave it puddled all over your antique you get the mess you found the next morning.

I will guess that the reason for adding the turpentine to the tung oil was to thin it so that the wood will absorb it more readily. This normally isn't a problem with tung oil, though, so I don't really see the need for the turpentine. Either way, however, slopping it on and letting it sit overnight isn't a good idea.

As for a solution to your problem, that's easy—have your husband strip it.

Q. About a year ago I refinished a walnut oval drop-leaf table that I had found at a yard sale. I stripped it out in my driveway, sanded it and finished it with tung oil. I have never been completely satisfied with the finish, because it looks dry in places and will water spot. I've got some vacation time coming up, and I want to do something to the table, since I like it so much but don't like the finish. Can I put a varnish directly over the old tung oil or do I have to strip it first?

A. What's going on here? There have been more letters about problems with tung-oil finishes than anything else lately. And it seems as if the story is the same each time—someone puts on tung oil, doesn't like it and decides to switch back to varnish. I can't believe that all those bottles and cans of tung oil are defective, so I'm going to assume the fault lies elsewhere.

Too many people see tung oil as being a fast and easy finish just because they don't have to use a brush. It is easy to apply, granted, but to get the same protection offered by a coat of varnish you are going to have to rub in at least six to ten coats of tung oil. That isn't the fault of the oil, although some manufacturers don't make that perfectly clear in their instructions.

A good friend of mine who builds walnut grandfather clocks swears by tung oil, but when pressed will admit that it doesn't begin to build up like standard varnish until somewhere after the fourteenth coat. He stops somewhere between twenty-five and thirty.

Before switching finishes, then, make sure you have given the tung oil a fair chance. It is a good finish, but like all finishes it must be applied properly. Before continuing with additional coats, though, clean your table thoroughly with mineral spirits and sand lightly with #220 sandpaper. If you are determined to varnish it, follow the same steps to clean it, but use a sanding sealer over the tung oil before applying your varnish.

Q. I'm writing to disagree with what you have said about using tung oil on antiques. You said you don't recommend it on table-tops and on oak furniture. I have been using nothing but tung oil on all my antiques for twelve years and have never had any problems with water spots or anything else. I think you're wrong in not telling your readers to use it. It's easier than messing with varnish, and you don't have any brush marks or drips. That's all I have to say except I think you're wrong.

A. So does Mr. Fornby, I would imagine, but I would guess neither one of you wears the same clothes to every different function you attend.

My point is this: with all the different woods we encounter and with all the different purposes for which we use these woods, it would be foolish to expect one finish to be best for every situation.

Tung oil has it advantages, some of which you mentioned, but it also falls short in other categories. It doesn't build up a protective finish as quickly as varnish, nor does it help much in filling the pores of the wood. By its nature, oil preserves better than it protects and it takes as many as eight to fifteen coats to equal the protection two coats of varnish provides.

Don't get me wrong. I don't use varnish exclusively either. I make it a point to choose my finish according to the type of wood, the type of use it will receive and the type of finish it had on it originally. If tung oil turns out to be the best, I use it. If not, I find something else.

Q. A friend of mine claims she stains and finishes small pieces she has stripped and sanded, with shoe polish. Have you heard of this being done or have you tried it? She claims it is much easier than messing with stains and varnishes.

A. I assume your friend was referring to paste shoe polishes, which are little more than colored wax. What she is doing, in effect, is applying wax to bare wood, a technique that is as old as any in wood finishing. Waxing wood is indeed simple and easy and involves very little mess or money. It has its drawbacks, however, and wax is not a popular finish today.

For a hard protective sheen, at least two coats of wax must be rubbed into the wood, each one buffed with a soft dry cloth. Even so, the wood is still susceptible to dents and scratches. The most obvious drawback to using wax shoe polish as a finish, though, is its tendency to become sticky and to attract dust and dirt. At that point the old wax must be removed with turpentine and new wax applied. Once a piece has had wax rubbed into the pores, it is not recommended that you switch to a varnish or lacquer finish later, for the wax can keep them from either sticking to the wood or drying properly.

Q. I happen to like the look, feel and smell of a linseed-oil finish, even if everyone else says it's too much work. It has been several years since I used boiled linseed oil and I would appreciate it if you could give me the formula and some simple directions for applying it.

A. Linseed-oil finishes have been greatly ignored in recent years since the advent of Danish oil and tung oil, which offer several advantages over this traditional finish. I agree with you, though, concerning the smell and feel of a linseed-oil finish, for it seems very appropriate for a true antique.

Dilute boiled linseed oil with an equal amount of mineral spirits to hasten the drying time and deepen the depth of absorption. Apply an even coat, but there's no need to flood the surface. Let the oil soak in for several minutes until the wood is saturated, then wipe off. Repeat this procedure a few hours later and again the next day.

Each day for the next week apply a coat of the mixture, let it soak in, wipe off the excess and rub briskly with a dry cloth. After a week of this, drop back to an application once a week. When you reach the point where the oil has attained the feel you desire, apply a coat of paste wax to the surface. Without the wax the linseed-oil finish will become sticky and will attract dust. Buff the paste wax to a satin finish.

If you decide later to add additional coats of oil to your piece, strip off the wax with mineral spirits and resume the procedure. The oil will provide a degree of protection against heat, water and alcohol in direct proportion to the number of coats that were applied.

Tip—If you like to use the time-tested formula of one-third varnish, one-third boiled linseed oil and one-third mineral spirits, heat it in a double-boiler setup until it is warm to the touch. It will flow better and will actually penetrate the wood more quickly warm than cold.

8 / All That Glitters...

So your antique has been stripped, sanded, repaired, re-glued, stained, filled, sealed and finished—you're all done, right? Wrong.

The first thing people are going to notice about anything you restore or refinish is the last thing you do anything about—the hardware. Handles, pulls, knobs, hinges, screws, castors, escutcheons, brackets, locks and whatever else isn't a natural part of the wood deserves as much attention as the wood itself. Spend two weeks working on an oak dresser and then stick the pulls back on without giving them so much as a second thought and you might just as well have never even started the project.

For the most part what we are talking about is simply cleaning that which is already there, although we do occasionally have to deal with the problems of missing or damaged hardware. Just as we wanted to avoid the "overrefinished" look in wood, the same goes for the hardware. It, too, has a patina that can be saved at the same time the hardware is being cleaned and polished, as this letter will help illustrate:

Q. We are in the business of refinishing antiques and have had good success with it. However, we cannot seem to discover a process for refinishing brass. Do you know of a good polishing method and a sealing method that works and does not discolor the metal?

A. I am not an advocate of highly polished brass on antiques, so I am not going to be able to offer advice on buffing wheels and rouges. A careful hand cleaning can eliminate enough of the tarnish to let the brass show through without making a hundred-year-old piece of hardware look like it was bought last week.

First you must determine if the brass has been coated with lacquer or wax to retard oxidation. If it has, this will also make it hard for you to clean and polish it. Bathe the brass in lacquer thinner to remove lacquer and mineral spirits to cut wax. Or you can take care of both problems at once by submerging it in paint-and-varnish remover. The stripper won't hurt the metal, but instead of using steel wool to clean it, substitute a rag. Polish with a soft cloth and a commercial brass cleaner to a mellow satin glow.

To hold the brass at this point, you can rub on a thin coat of paste wax. It will not discolor the brass, but it will keep the air from tarnishing it.

Tip—Don't make the mistake of overpolishing brass hardware or brass and copper accessories. Antiques are both meant and expected to look their age. Overpolished pieces look like reproductions and can actually be worth less than they were before you attacked them with your electric drill and a buffing attachment.

Q. How would you go about cleaning old drawer handles? On a dresser of mine that once belonged to my great-aunt, the pulls look like gold tin that turned green. The handles are held in place by two eyelet bolts that go all the way through the front of the drawer.

A. You can remove the hardware from the drawer by taking off the two nuts that hold the eyelet bolts in place. This should make the cleaning process easier. If the brass isn't tarnished too badly, any commercial metal cleaner should work well.

On more stubborn areas, try a mixture of vinegar and lemon

juice (more vinegar than lemon juice) and a soft cloth. Afterwards, return to the commercial polish to shine them up.

Tip—The old method of cleaning brass called for a slice of lemon dipped in salt. The acid in the fruit attacks the tarnish while the salt provides a mild abrasive. If you can't lick 'em, use 'em.

Tip—Baby-food jars work well for keeping hardware, hinges and small parts from getting lost while you are refinishing your antiques. Use masking tape to label each jar. If you're not currently in the baby business, another cheap and convenient way is to drop them in a regular envelope, seal the flap and identify the contents on the outside.

Q. We have just bought an oak buffet that had been refinished by the dealer we bought it from. It must have been painted, because we can still see bits of paint in the crevices of the hardware. The dealer also must have varnished the hardware when he varnished

Antique hardware can be stripped of paint or old varnish by either brushing on a coat of paint-and-varnish remover or immersing it in a coffee can of used stripper. As you can see by this photograph, the right half of this old drawer pull has been stripped of several layers of paint. Rather than using even fine steel wool to scrub off the loosened finish, however, switch to an old toothbrush, which won't scratch the metal—but don't plan on being able to use it for your teeth again.

the rest of the buffet, because it has a finish over it. I tried cleaning one of the pulls, but of course it did no good. Can I strip the varnish off the hardware without harming it?

A. Certainly, so long as it is all metal. You'll be pleasantly surprised when you see that the stripper will take the paint out of the crevices of the pulls as well. Drop the hardware in the stripper and, a few hours later, pull it out, rinse it off, polish and put it back on the buffet.

Q. I am restoring an old steamer trunk that has a lot of metal pieces—a lock and latch, corner pieces, straps, etc.—most of which are very rusty. What do you recommend for cleaning it?

A. Naval jelly and #000 steel wool.

Q. Before I polish the brass hardware on a walnut rolltop desk I just bought (it doesn't need refinishing, just a good cleaning), I want to know what to use to keep it all shiny afterwards. Will varnish work?

A. Varnish is difficult to brush on—or apply any way for that matter—so I wouldn't recommend it. Instead, get an aerosol can of clear lacquer from a paint store and mist the brass with it. It won't take much, so go easy on the spraying.

Tip—A piece of Styrofoam works well for holding hardware while it dries. Simply stick one end in it and spray.

Q. I have just inherited a brass bed that is in very good condition except that it is slightly tarnished. My mother told me that she could remember cleaning and polishing it dozens of times, and each time it would start tarnishing a few days later. I know I have seen brass beds in antique shops that weren't tarnished and wonder if you could tell me how they do it?

A. I can't say for sure, obviously, but I'll assume they were coated with lacquer. A fine misting will seal the brass and slow down the tarnishing action, but for something as large as a bed I would suggest that you get an estimate from a professional with full-scale spray equipment rather than trying it yourself with aerosol cans.

Q. I have an oak drop-front desk that has small glass doors in the part down below the drop front. The desk is in excellent condition and we use it every day, but there is something about it that has always bothered me. There is no knob on the doors and really no way to get them open without sticking a screwdriver or the end of a pair of scissors in the keyhole to act as a pull.

The door on this secretary-bookcase never had a pull; the key is intended to serve as both a handle and a means of operating the lock.

Should there be a knob on the doors? I have looked for some indication that one used to be there but can find nothing. I'm afraid someone is going to scratch the finish if we have to keep opening them this way.

A. Many of the desks, bookcases and cupboards from the Victorian era never had knobs on the doors, but were opened simply by pulling on the key that was left in the keyhole. Furniture makers of the period were intent, it seems, to have several locks and keys on every piece of furniture and used the keys as knobs as well.

What you need to do is find a locksmith who has on hand blanks of the old-style keys. Slip one of these into the keyhole, turn it upside down to catch on the mechanism (it need not actually lock the doors) and use it as a means of opening them.

. . .

A more perplexing problem arises when your antique comes to you minus some or all of its original hardware. Early furniture manufacturers used so many different styles and designs of hardware that it is a rare and wonderful day when you find a legitimate old piece to complete your set. Even though the odds are stacked against that happening, never stop looking under tables at flea markets and in the buckets and boxes of miscellaneous hardware all antique dealers seem to have.

In the meantime, with the renewed interest in proper antique restoration, a number of companies specializing in reproduction hardware have sprung up. Naturally some reproductions are very good and others, quite frankly, stink. You'll spot the difference immediately; cheaper hardware is lighter, looks shiny and tinny and bends under only the slightest pressure. Unfortunately, you are going to have to rely somewhat on trial and error to separate the good companies from the bad; talk to antique dealers and refinishers, however, and they may be able to make a few recommendations. You'll also need to know:

Q. What is meant by the term "bore"?

A. Unless you're referring to some of the antique snobs we all know and love, I'll guess you mean "bore" as it refers to drawer hardware.

If a piece of hardware has a 3-inch bore, then the distance between the two shafts that pass through the holes in the drawer front will be 3 inches. The bore, then, is the distance between these two shafts. For most pieces the hardware bore is either 2, 2½ or 3 inches, but make sure you know which size you need before placing an order or making a purchase.

Tip—Take time to send away for all the hardware, specialty tool and reproduction catalogs advertised in antique and hobby magazines. Inside them you'll find everything from odd-sized hinges to spool-cabinet pulls to porcelain castors.

Tip—If you, too, dislike the "new" look of reproduction hardware, several companies are now offering an antiquing solution that will quickly tarnish shiny new hardware to make it look more like legitimate old pieces. Check for hardware companies advertising in antique-related magazines.

Q. I ordered a pair of teardrop pulls from one of the nationally known reproduction hardware companies on the East Coast for a walnut commode I am refinishing. The pulls arrived in less than

Can you identify the original, the reproduction and the reproduction that has been artificially tarnished? The new one is in the middle, the original is on the left and the one on the right is the same age as the one in the middle, but it was treated with an antiquing solution from Heirloom Brass Co. (see Chapter 10 for address).

three weeks and were of extremely high quality. Both the brass plate and the wood piece are highly polished, but now my two original pulls look drab in comparison. What can I use to polish both the brass plate and the wood teardrop on the two older pulls to match the new ones?

A. Personally, I would approach the problem from the opposite point of view. Rather than trying to make your old pulls look new, consider attempting to age the reproductions to simulate your eighty-to-one-hundred-year-old pulls. In the end, your dresser will look more natural and less like you had had to replace all four pulls.

To take the gloss off the lacquered wood, rub the teardrop with #000 steel wool. The same will work on the brass plate. If your originals are badly tarnished, fine steel wool and a commercial metal polish will bring back some of their original shine. Nicks and scratches on the wood portion can be touched up with black paint or shoe polish, then sprayed with clear lacquer. By cleaning up the old pulls and toning down the new, you should be able to come up with a set that look like they have spent their entire lives together.

Tip—To instantly age new screws so that they blend in with the originals in your restoration projects, heat the heads with a cigarette lighter or small torch, then submerge in water. Let cool completely before handling.

Q. I purchased a set of reproduction hardware from an antique dealer at an out-of-state flea market. I want to put it on an oak commode I have had for several years, but have done nothing with recently because it came with no hardware. My problem is that the new hardware is attached from inside the drawer, as was the old, but the new screws aren't long enough to go all the way through the wood and into the hardware.

I have looked in hardware stores for a similar but longer screw, but can't find anything just like it. Is there a place I can order a set or do you have another solution?

A. I have a solution that may also solve a problem you haven't even anticipated.

Antique drawer fronts, which the screws must go through, are generally thicker than the standard ¾-inch lumber we are used to today. To give the screw additional length without changing it, simply countersink the screwhole from the inside of the drawer. If you take a ½-inch drill and deepen the hole just ¼ inch, the head of the screw will then be flush with the inside of the drawer and the threads will extend farther toward the front.

This not only will give your hardware something to grab onto, but will keep you from snagging either your hand or your clothes on the head of the screw as you take them out of the drawer.

Tip—Keep a special can or box for miscellaneous screws, washers, nuts and bolts, etc., that you either end up with or find. In a short time you'll have an assortment that will save you several trips to the hardware store in search of one special piece.

Get into the habit of picking up and saving odds and ends of old hardware. Auctions, yard sales, basements and garages are gold mines of pulls, knobs, locks and castors—which sooner or later you are going to need in one of your restoration projects.

Q. My husband and I are in the middle of a major refinishing project—a four-door oak icebox that we are going to use as a liquor cabinet in our family room. We are almost done, and I have started cleaning the latches and hinges but have a problem. It appears that they were plated with something like silver or nickel, but there is more plating gone than left. I can see on the backs and in the places where the plating has flaked off that the hardware is actually brass.

Would it be alright for us to take the rest of the plating off and polish the brass? If so, will stripper take the plating off?

A. It wasn't unusual for companies to offer their iceboxes with either nickel-plated or solid brass hinges and latches, so, yes, you could go ahead as you suggested. The only problem is that stripper doesn't usually remove plating; anything like a wire wheel or even steel wool is going to do serious damage to the brass underneath. Electroplating companies have the chemicals necessary to dissolve the plating, but it is difficult, first, to find them and, second, to find someone there who will handle a job that small.

Tip—One of our readers writes: "The person who wrote and asked how to remove the plating from old icebox hinges has two easy options open to her.

"Most oven cleaners have the warning not to spray it on plated surfaces and they mean it. Spray it on your icebox hardware and it will peel the plating right off.

"The second is even easier. Take it to an electroplater and he will strip it for a very reasonable fee."

Q. I recently bought a small two-drawer antique walnut table. Each drawer has two mushroom pulls on it, but the cap of one of the pulls has either been broken or chipped off.

The pulls all screw into the wood; no nails or wooden pegs were used. What should I do to repair the wooden pull, the cap of which is about half gone? I have a walnut pull like it, but it doesn't screw in like the originals.

Should I cut the damaged pull off the drawer (it won't unscrew without breaking) and glue on the new pull, or try to glue a piece of wood on the damaged pull?

A. My first reaction is always to try to save as much of the original as possible, but it seems as if you have several alternatives.

Find a small piece of walnut similar in grain and color to your damaged pull. File and sand it and the pull until the two come together with enough surface contact to glue. Glue, clamp for twenty-four hours, then sand to the proper shape.

If for some reason the repair won't hold, you have three choices: replace the original with the pull you now have, replace the pull with a duplicate made on a lathe, or live with it the way it is. Unless the new pull you now have is an exact duplicate, I would lean toward having an identical one made.

Tip—If, for any reason, you choose to remove or change any hardware—castors, pulls, locks, whatever—on an antique, tie together and label the originals (if they are originals) and keep them in a drawer or somehow attached to the piece. Someday you or the next owner may want to return it to its original condition.

9 / Special Problems

R egardless of how well we love categories—Chippendale, Shaker, Eastlake, Empire, Mission—not every antique fits neatly into a designated slot. The same goes for problems with antiques, for not every dilemma automatically classifies itself as being a question of stripping, sanding, staining or finishing. Rather than ignore either those antiques or their special problems that defy classification—for many times these are of unusual interest—we have given them their own chapter. And if this isn't a "special problem" then I don't know what is:

Q. My mother is so stubborn I could shake her! She has two lovely walnut parlor tables with bluish marble tops that she is determined to have cut down to coffee-table size. To her they are just old wood tables that were in her home when she was a child and don't mean that much to her.

I told her nobody would shorten them for her because it

would ruin their value, but she claims she'll do it herself. The more I argue, the more stubborn she gets. I offered to buy them from her at full market value, but she refuses. She says she likes them, but not so tall.

Right now we're not talking and the rest of the family thinks we're both crazy. I'm hoping that if I show her your column she'll reconsider, so please answer as soon as possible.

A. Well, we can assume that you have used all the standard arguments regarding drastic alterations to antiques that permanently decrease their value and destroy their aesthetic beauty, depriving future generations of their use, etc., etc., to no avail. We can also assume that since the two of you are no longer speaking, another method of communication should be employed.

First, find a friend or family member whose opinions your mother values and explain the situation to him or her. If this column can help, great, but chances are she will be more willing to listen to an unbiased observer. Second, see if you can locate two other pieces of furniture that will fill the need for two low coffee tables. Check within the family first, then antique shops and furniture stores.

Finally, if none of these work, steal the tables. With no priors and a sympathetic judge, you shouldn't get more than six months probation.

Q. Why is it that antique end tables and coffee tables are so hard to find? We have been looking for a low table to go in front of our couch for months now, and a friend of mine wants a pair of oak end tables to go beside hers. Didn't they make them or does everybody just hold on to theirs?

A. Most of our popular and available antiques come from the Victorian era, and it seems that coffee tables and end tables, at least at the low height we are accustomed to, weren't popular then (probably because they didn't have television to watch). For that reason we find many library tables and even round oak dining room tables have been cut down to set in front of or beside a modern couch. I don't want to even hint that you should

Six-drawer spool cabinets are but one type of antique that can be adapted for modern use without doing any damage to its original form. The drawers offer additional storage for magazines, coasters and placemats.

consider doing this, but you might be able to find one that has already been cut down—that is, if you don't decide to have it raised back up and use it in your kitchen.

Instead, consider looking for antiques out of the traditional mold to use as coffee or end tables, such as spool cabinets, card catalogues or small trunks. The best example of this I have ever seen was a 1920s apartment-size oak icebox that stood less than 2 feet tall, had a flat top and two doors on the top rather than the side. It made a darling coffee table and gave its owner storage space for coasters, magazines and blankets.

. . .

Mirrors have always been popular, thus we find many of our antiques such as dressers, buffets, hall seats and secretaries come equipped with them—and some corresponding problems:

Q. I read in a refinishing book written by a well-known author that antique mirrors should never be resilvered. I have a Victorian oak secretary with a small beveled mirror that is in such bad shape that you can't even see yourself in it. Does this mean I would be decreasing the value of my secretary if I had the mirror resilvered?

A. In all likelihood, no.

The opinion you are referring to has been quoted to me many times, but too often the emphasis is put solely on the word "mirror" and the adjective "antique" is ignored. Antique mirrors are as different from old mirrors as a true antique is from an old piece of furniture.

Although silver has always been the primary coating used in mirror production, the method of applying it has changed over the years. Prior to 1840, mercury was used in the process, and it is chiefly these antique mercury-silvered mirrors that are sought by collectors, regardless of their condition. A reputable mirror resilverer will be able to tell at first glance whether or not your mirror was silvered prior to 1840 and can help you determine how it can best be preserved. In a piece such as yours, I would judge that a good resilvering would do more to enhance its value than would leaving it in its present unusable condition.

Q. I've been trying to find someone who resilvers mirrors for a reasonable price and have come to the conclusion there isn't anybody. I used to know three or four shops that did it years ago, but now I'm told most of them went out of business when the price of silver went up. The one that is left sure hasn't dropped his prices now that silver is back where it should be. What's so tough about resilvering mirrors that nobody wants to do it and the few who do charge so much?

A. Nothing, except that the price of your materials is determined by a pair of brothers in Texas, you have to work with wet glass and dangerous chemicals and even the tiniest flaw shows up like a wart on the end of your nose. And your profits? They go into Band-Aids.

Q. Do you know of any easy method to take the silvering off mirrors without scraping? Also could you explain how silvering is done, and do you know of a mirror company that reproduces fancy beveled mirrors?

A. The easiest way I have found to take old silvering off mirrors is to take them to a professional mirror resilverer. The process is quite complicated and, more important, quite dangerous. Mirror resilvering involves everything from toxic chemicals to expensive equipment and valuable silver and is not recommended for anyone but the professionals.

Briefly, old silvering is removed using the quite toxic nitric acid, the glass surface is prepared and raw silver, after being turned into a liquid solution through the use of other toxic chemicals, is applied to the glass at a temperature of 240 degrees. Old glass has been known to literally explode upon impact of the hot silver solution, sending shards of glass into the face of the resilverer.

And as if that weren't enough to deter you, consider the fluctuation and instability of the price of your main ingredient—silver. In short, mirror resilvering is meant only for the professionals, and most of them will tell you it isn't worth the risk at any price.

As for a source of beveled mirrors, check with your local glass shops. They should know where in your area standard mirrors can be cut and beveled to your specifications.

Tip—When tapping in brads to hold a mirror in a frame, tape a cloth over the side of your hammer to avoid scratching the

coating on the back of the glass. Or you can do the same by holding a piece of cardboard between your hammer and the glass. It can keep a slip of the hand from destroying a valuable old mirror, or a freshly resilvered one.

. . .

And speaking of damage, nothing puts The Fear in an antique-lover faster than the word "mover." It doesn't matter if you're doing it yourself, having friends help out or calling in the professionals, you're going to be a wreck; but let's hope your antiques won't be.

Q. My husband and I have collected antiques for several years and are now preparing to make our first major move. We are going to hire professional movers and are quite nervous about the possibility of having some of our antiques damaged.

One in particular we are concerned about is a secretary with curved-glass doors. How should it be transported? Should the glass be removed? Do you have any suggestions that might help us avoid any damage?

A. There are several precautions you can take to protect your antiques, but you have to realize that most of the responsibility will be out of your hands and in those, quite literally, of your movers. Make sure, then, that you hire the services of a reputable firm. In the event damage does occur, you will have better luck getting both cooperation and cash for repairs from a company that has been in business for several years and works in the area you are moving to as well as that which you are leaving.

As for the antiques themselves, there are some special precautions you can take. Remove the curved glass doors from your secretary, for instance, and pack them separately. Do not remove the glass from the frame, however; the support is essential. Cut strips of inner tube to form giant rubber bands to keep doors closed and dresser drawers from falling out. Clearly mark boxes and pieces that have to be transported right side up. Above all else, be there when the pieces are both loaded and unloaded. Don't be a pest, but be around to make sure a fragile antique isn't being treated like a used refrigerator.

Tip—Unless you are extremely fortunate, odds are that sooner or later you and your antiques are going to run into some furniture movers lacking a fine appreciation for antiques. While dents, scratches and such can be repaired, one of the most damaging and difficult to repair accidents involves a piece of wood being knocked off an antique and never recovered. If you see that one of the legs on a chair has a piece missing, check inside the van before the movers leave. In fact, have them sweep out the van while you stand by with a cardboard box to catch it all rather than letting them pull away with a slice of veneer or piece of claw foot still inside. It may seem a bit crazy, but it's worth it.

Q. We have been told by our friends that we need to have our antiques appraised in order for them to be covered by our insurance policy. We do have several nice antiques, most of which were always in one of our two families, but I don't know anything about having an appraisal done. Could you tell me how appraisers charge, who you have do it and whether they tell you how much a piece would sell for or how much it would cost to replace it?

A. It is always a good idea to check your insurance policy or with your agent to see that your antiques are considered "antiques" and not simply "household furnishings." Some companies require a separate rider listing each antique and its appraised value.

If this is the case, check the Yellow Pages of your phone book under Antique Dealers for persons also advertising an appraisal service. There are at least three major organizations qualified professional appraisers can belong to: the American Society of Appraisers, the Appraisers Association of America and the Mid-America Appraisers Association, so you might want to watch for them in your search through the ads.

Ask any appraisers you speak to whether they charge on a per item basis or at an hourly rate and whether or not the latter includes research time. You should also indicate whether you are interested in having your antiques appraised at their market value or their insurance value. To some there may not be a difference, but many times there is.

Q. I have a White treadle sewing machine that is over one hundred years old. Could you give me any information on it or tell me where I could get someone to appraise it, since I want to sell it? Thank you.

A. The White brand of sewing machine was very popular for many, many years; in fact, it is not unusual to find them still in working condition and being used daily.

For that reason, they generally do not command high prices on the open market. In addition, it is awfully hard to find a secondary use for them without simply turning one into a table for plants. The key to any value a treadle sewing machine might have will be twofold: the machine itself should work and the thin oak veneer must be in excellent condition. As far as getting it accurately appraised, call some of your local antique dealers and ask who in your area can give you an appraisal that will enable you to determine how much you can expect to get for the machine when you go to sell it.

Q. Do partial pieces of antique furniture have any value? I have the bottom of an old kitchen cabinet and several old dressers that have had the mirrors removed. I'm not thinking about discarding any of them, since I use them anyway, but I wondered if they have any antique value.

A. Partial antiques are much like a good glove waiting to find its mate: It's too good to throw away, but what do you do with it? I guess the answer is you should keep them, use them, but don't do anything to them you wouldn't do to a complete antique. Hopefully someday they, too, will find their mate—and their full value.

. . .

Although problems with caning are primarily confined to chairs and rockers, this is an area of antique restoration that has spawned several questions. A few of the more typical should shed some light on caning and its role in the restoration process:

Q. I know there are two or three (maybe more) different types of cane available. How do I go about deciding which one to use in my chairs?

A. You don't. The chairs do.

Chair cane is most often found in two forms: strand and web. And while the two techniques used to install them are drastically different, the finished products look very similar. It will be your chairs, however, that will determine which type you will need to use.

If your chair has a series of holes drilled around the opening in the seat, then you must use strand cane, which consists of long, loose fibers that are woven one at a time. Chairs with a groove routed around the opening instead of holes call for web cane, which is simply prewoven strand cane. It comes from the factory in rolls ranging from 12 inches to over 20 inches wide and up to 50 feet long.

Both types are soaked before being woven or installed; when the water evaporates the strands shrink and form a tight seat. Strand cane is less expensive to purchase, but takes longer to install because it must be woven. Web cane, on the other hand, is more expensive to buy, but can be installed in less than thirty minutes. Both, however, have a similar life expectancy of about twenty-five years.

The chair on the left with the groove cut in the seat requires web, or "pressed," cane, which comes prewoven and is held in place with a strip called the spline. The chair on the right is drilled for strand, or "loose," cane; the pegs hold the strands taut until they are tied underneath.

Q. My husband finally decided to change the burned-out light bulb in our kitchen last week, but in doing so, he managed to put his foot through one of my caned-seat oak chairs. He immediately went out and bought some cane from one of our local antique dealers, so I could recane it before our weekend guests arrived two days later.

I finished the caning in time, but now I have one chair seat that is obviously new and three that look considerably older. Is there a trick to aging the new cane?

A. Instant aging isn't a process our society puts special emphasis on today, but it is possible to soften the obviously new look of bleached cane.

Before embarking on the process, though, I would recommend that you check to see if your three other chairs are soon to need recaning as well. If they are beginning to break, it would be best to cane them now rather than later attempting to match them to the one you just finished.

Cane has a rounded, glossy side that resists stains and a flat, dull side that has just the opposite characteristic. It is possible, however, to get the sealed side to accept some stain in an attempt to age it or to match it to the other chair seats. Select a penetrating wood stain as close as possible to the color you want (usually a golden oak or very light walnut); test it on some unused cane.

Brush the stain on the back of the cane first, then do the same for the front. Let it stand until a sufficient amount has been absorbed, then carefully wipe off the excess. Although it isn't usually recommended for cane, you'll need to mist it with spray lacquer to keep the stain on the cane seat and not *your* seat.

Q. I found at a garage sale a small bedroom rocker with a caned seat and back, both of which are in good shape. The problem, though, is that the finish is flaking off the wood in places and it needs refinishing. Can I refinish the rocker without having to recane it as well?

A. Yes, if you're careful.

Regular paint-and-varnish remover can weaken the strands, so you're going to want to strip your rocker with either lacquer thinner or denatured alcohol if at all possible (see Chapter 4). Even then you're going to need to be careful about not getting excessive amounts of the solvents on the cane. Sanding will be tedious, as will staining and varnishing, since you won't want to get anything on the strands. The end result is worth the bother, however, since you will both save the cost of a new seat and will have a rocking chair that looks its age.

. . .

Veneer problems always seem to scare everybody away, and understandably so. Once veneer is damaged—be it chipped, cracked, warped or bubbled—any repairs invariably show. And if you think getting new cane to match old is tough, try blending new veneer with 150-year-old wood. There are some problems, though, that don't have to be taken to the professionals, as these letters prove:

Q. Should veneer be repaired before or after the stripping process?

A. Under most circumstances, it is safer to reglue loose veneer before applying stripper. Even though you won't be using water as a rinse (it dissolves the old veneer glues, remember?—use lacquer thinner or denatured alcohol instead), you will be less apt to snag and break loose pieces. You also avoid the problem encountered when stripper residue prevents the glue from adhering to the wood.

If you do your veneer patching before you strip you can also get a jump on staining and blending the new to fit with the old by smearing the old finish and stain over the new patch to make it appear as much like the original as possible.

Q. I just bought an oak dresser at an auction over the weekend, knowing that there was a bubble in the veneer on the top. The bubble is not broken, but I want to fix it before it breaks. Can this be done without refinishing the dresser? The finish is in excellent shape and I really don't want to lose the lovely patina. Can you tell me how to repair it myself?

A. Certainly—and it won't require any refinishing.

Take either a single-edged razor blade or a hobby knife and make a single incision in the direction of the grain along the top of the bubble. The incision should go not quite the length of the bubble and only through the veneer and not the wood underneath.

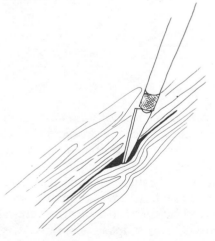

Eliminating a bubble in veneer. Slice bubble in the direction of the grain, then depress one side with your knife to insert the glue. Press down with your finger along the incision to force the glue back into the void, then repeat for the other side of the bubble.

Depress one side of the bubble and either inject or, using the tip of your knife, slide some epoxy under the raised half. Repeat for the other side. Using your fingertip, press down along the incision, forcing the glue back into the far reaches of the bubble. As excess glue comes out of the incision wipe it off with a rag dampened with lacquer thinner.

Since the bubble appeared in the middle of your dresser top you won't be able to hold it down with a C-clamp. Instead, lay a piece of wax paper over the incision, then stack enough weight on it to push the bubble down flat. The wax paper will keep the glue that is forced out from sticking to the weight. If weights stacked directly on the veneer bubble are not enough to hold it in place, rig a "teeter-totter" clamp (see illustration below). Let the glue have twenty-four hours to dry, then remove the weight and wax paper. The dried glue will come off with only a little pressure from your razor blade. If the edges of the veneer have overlapped, trim until both are flush, then touch up with stain and a little varnish or tung oil.

If weights stacked directly on a veneer bubble or a patch are not enough to hold it in place while glue dries, rig a "teeter-totter" clamp, using a block of wood and piece of wax paper over the repair, two strips of wood spanning the width and two C-clamps.

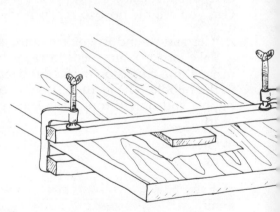

Q. I read with great interest an earlier column of yours in which you explained how to repair a veneer bubble. My problem is a bit more severe. I stripped a mahogany-veneered buffet this summer and left it in my garage while I went on vacation.

When I returned I found that it had rained and my roof had leaked. Naturally the buffet, minus any finish, was directly under the hole. The water had evaporated by that time, but the veneer had blistered and ruptured in two long strips. Each bubble is nearly 6 inches long, an inch or more wide and is raised nearly an inch above the rest of the wood.

I tried the method you gave in the earlier column, but the veneer is brittle, and rather than lie down, it breaks when pressure is applied. Is there any way this can be fixed or will I have to reveneer the entire top?

A. It does sound as if you have a real problem on your hands, but it might be possible to make suitable repairs. If not, little is lost if you later decide to reveneer the top.

The water did two things to your buffet. First, it dissolved the glue holding the veneer to the top boards. Second, it caused the veneer to swell and warp. Unfortunately, when the water evaporated, the glue rehardened before the veneer returned to its previous position.

To soften the veneer bubbles, moisten them with a damp cloth. Wet a towel, wring it out and lay it over the affected area. Don't leave it unattended for long, however, for you want to soften the veneer but not cause it to swell any more.

Once the veneer is pliable, press the bubbles back in place and glue with epoxy as outlined previously. If it is necessary, with a new hobby knife carefully trim any excess until the edges join.

P.S. Regardless of the condition of your roof, it is not a good idea to strip a piece of its finish unless you can complete the restoration work shortly thereafter.

Tip—The insides of dresser drawers and old picture frames are good sources of items of historical importance. Don't discard any old newspaper until you have had an opportunity to thoroughly assess its contents.

Q. I started my own business thirty-seven years ago and am now semiretired with some extra time on my hands. I have refinished furniture as a hobby for nearly nine years and am thinking about taking in some refinishing jobs that my friends have been asking me to do for a long time now. What I'm not sure of is how to charge. All the work I've done before was either for our home or for one of our children, so I haven't any experience at charging for my work. Do you have any suggestions?

A. If you've had your own business for nearly forty years you've probably had more experience with people and pricing than any professional refinisher in town.

To begin with, contact some of the refinishers in your area and ask what their hourly rate is or what they normally charge for refinishing a straight-back chair or regluing a rocker, for instance. This will give you an idea what your friends would be paying if they took their work to a professional shop.

The major consideration, however, is going to be your time and how highly you value it. Materials will seem a little costly at first, but you'll find that with a limited number of projects, each can of stripper, stain or varnish will last quite a while. Most of your investment will be labor, and so long as you can work out of your own home or garage you can keep your overhead down.

Let me make one suggestion. Regardless of what you charge, make sure everyone involved has at least a general idea of what the project is going to cost before you start. Many people still think they can have a chair refinished for five or ten dollars and don't realize that it costs nearly that much just for a quart of varnish. You'll save several friendships if money is discussed first and not last.

Tip—If you find yourself moving your refinishing projects around alone, save yourself some lower-back problems by constructing a simple furniture dolly. A couple of 2 x 4s, a piece of ¾-inch plywood and four swivel rubber wheels is all it takes to save yourself an expensive trip to the hospital.

Q. My husband and I have been collecting antiques for almost thirty years now and have a house, basement and garage full. In another year we will both be retired and are thinking about setting up a booth at a couple of antique shows in the summer for both the fun of it and to supplement our retirement income. Are shows doing very well these days, and would you recommend this over setting up a regular shop?

A. Like all aspects of the antique business, including setting up a regular shop, shows are a gamble. You invest a booth rental fee, your cost of packing and transporting your goods, your time in setting up, watching and dismantling your display and your meals and lodging during the show. What you hope to reap are sales, connections and, of course, fun.

I would recommend that you begin by attending even more shows, but not during peak times. Try to catch a few exhibitors when they aren't busy and ask them how things are going. Compare booth layouts and try to determine which ones people naturally walk into and which ones make it difficult for customers to enter.

Talk to your local dealers and find out about nearby shows. The best ones are filled several months in advance, though you may be able to get in on short notice if there is a last-minute cancellation. Discuss booth rentals with show organizers and ask for sample floor plans and contracts.

I would also recommend that you start by doing a show near home, as this will cut down on your lodging and transportation costs and will enable you to run home for things you forget (like the time I forgot the price tags). You'll learn a great deal that first time out. Good shows are fun, not just because you can come home with a fistful of dollars, but because of the many interesting people you meet and the friendships you will form with other exhibitors. As for the bad shows, well, I'll let you describe them to us later.

Q. I am having problems finding a dependable refinisher. I have a very ornate oval table that had a rose marble top on it. While in transit the table fell and broke. The marble, of course, is in about three large sections now, and the wood part of the table is also broken.

I cannot mend the table myself, and my problem is that I have already had it to several places without its being fixed. One man had it for eight months and did nothing to it. He told me the table was hand carved from several types of wood and definitely was worth fixing. But then he never got around to fixing it.

My next attempt also failed. The man again kept the table, saying he would fix it, but then called to say he didn't have the proper clamps, but he was very willing to buy the table or swap me for it. I went and got it instead. I'm almost afraid to take it anywhere else for fear of losing pieces or of being cheated. If you could give me any advice I would appreciate it.

A. Choosing a restoration shop is not as easy as just letting your fingers do the walking. As in all professions, there are a variety of skilled and unskilled, equipped and unequipped, and ethical and unethical refinishers wanting your business.

I'm sure there is a competent refinisher in your area who is not anxious to cheat you out of your table and who can properly repair the damage it has experienced. The Yellow Pages are a good place to start, but follow that up by asking your friends who they have had good experience with. If you are new in the area, call some of the antique dealers and ask whom they would recommend.

Once you have the names of a few restorers, call to get such basic information as their hours, their location, the types of antiques they work on and their current backlog. Visit the shops to get a feel for their work. You can tell a great deal about their craftsmanship just by their organization and how they treat you and the pieces in the shop.

Don't hesitate to ask for references and a written estimate. Discuss, as well, how long the repairs should take and, if necessary, set a date by which the work is to be completed. A week or so before the date arrives, call to make sure the deadline will not be missed. You'll find a little extra effort is worth it, not only in dollars and cents, but in eliminated worry as well. A good refinisher is like a good doctor or a reliable mechanic: the more they get to know you, the easier it is for them to know just what you want.

10 / Sources

Working with what we've got in front of us, be it a piece of hardware, a broken rocker or six layers of latex paint, naturally presents us with a few problems, but we expect and, hopefully, enjoy that aspect of antique restoration. What becomes frustrating, though, is not being able to locate the parts, tools and materials we need to complete our restoration. The search for missing pieces never seems to end, for just when we find a complete set of icebox hardware, we buy a Hoosier cupboard needing a sugar cannister, and by the time we find that we've already started looking for a set of hip-huggers for a walnut chair and once we're that far into antique collecting we might as well resign ourselves to spending a good portion of our lives poking through buckets of hardware and boxes of junk in search of "just one more hinge."

So here are some of the questions we encountered most often and at least a few answers that might be of help to you:

One of the fortunate side effects of the surging interest in antique restoration is the rapid growth in the number of companies offering quality reproduction hardware.

Q. Where can I find antique hardware, such as drawer pulls and knobs, for my refinishing projects? I'm working on two things at once, a dresser and a drop-front desk, and they both are missing some parts.

A. Sources—reliable sources—for genuine antique hardware are difficult to find. And those who do find them are reluctant to share that information and for obvious reasons. The difference in value between two identical antiques, one with original hardware and one with reproductions, can amount to a considerable sum.

Auctions are one source for old hardware, but I hesitate to call them reliable. Check boxes in and around the tools that were hauled out of the barn, garage or basement rather than those near the furniture. If the owner kept things like old castors, pulls and hinges, they would more often than not be with the nails, tools and junk.

Flea markets are another good source, but here again don't expect to find much hardware on top of the tables with the antiques. Poke around underneath, being careful, of course, not to mistake the leg of a dealer for an old fireplace iron.

Antique dealers and restoration shops generally have the best selection of old hardware simply because in their business it is a necessity. For that same reason they are reluctant to part with it, unless you make them an offer they can't refuse.

Q. I have an oak highboy dresser with, would you believe, six drawers, none of which has any hardware on it. The dealer who sold it to me told me he bought it at an auction all complete, but when he went to get it at the end of the sale someone had stolen all the brass hardware off the drawers. I can see the outline on the wood where the pulls went, but I know I'll never find the originals again.

Could you tell me where I could order a complete set?

A. There must be over a dozen different companies reproducing hardware for antiques ranging from Chippendale sideboards to oak filing cabinets, most of which advertise on a regular basis in the major antique newspapers and magazines across the country. I'll just mention a few to get you started: Horton Brasses, Box 95, Nooks Hill Road, Cromwell, CT 06416; Heirloom Brass Co., Box 146, Dundas, MN 55019; and WSI Distributors, Box 1235, St. Charles, MO 63301.

Q. I am seeking information on making or buying pierced tin panels for a pie safe I acquired some time ago. It has two openings in each front door 5½ inches wide by 31¾ inches long and an opening in each side that is 6 inches by 31¾ inches. If I can't buy panels like this already pierced, then I need sources for unpierced tin and examples of patterns. Do you know of any books or publications on this subject?

A. I mentioned in an earlier column that I had recently seen some information on making your own pierced tin panels and an ad for a company that sold them, but could not recall where I had spotted them. Luckily one of our readers saw the same article and had a better memory than your columnist.

He wrote to tell us that the magazine *Early American Life* carried a detailed article by Barbara Radcliffe Rogers in the June 1980 issue entitled "Pierced Tin for Kitchen Cabinets." The article is quite good, as the author explains how she and her husband take rubbings from original tins, make patterns and punch out the designs.

In the same issue, but on page 77 of the classified advertising, you can find an ad for a do-it-yourself kit available from the Sobys, P.O. Box 180, Western Springs, IL 60558. I haven't seen the kit, but the ad mentions tin, tools, instructions and patterns. If you try it, we'd be interested in learning of your experiences.

Q. I am having a problem with a pie safe that I am restoring that must be a common one. The piece has sixteen tins, the bottom four of which have rusted through. A local tinsmith will punch replacements from new tin for a reasonable price, but the new tin is so shiny that it will never match the other originals. Is there a way to antique or distress new tin to make it match more closely with the older tins?

A. That all depends. If your local tinsmith is using galvanized tin, which is the most common and the most widely used by tinsmiths in their work, the answer is no.

Professionals in the antique business who reproduce tins for pie safes use a type of metal called tinplate, which can be antiqued using an acid bath or, believe it or not, naval jelly. Unfortunately, tinplate is difficult to locate in small quantities, so you may have to turn to the professionals advertising in antique publications for a source of suitable metal. One of the largest suppliers for refinishers is Country Accents, Box 293, Stockton, NH 08559. Their catalogue can be ordered for two dollars.

Q. My wife's grandparents' pictures have been given to us. They are in large oval frames, but one of the frames has the glass missing. The glass is a large oval and is convex. I have gone to all the local glass shops and they can't get the glass. The picture is also convex, so a flat piece of glass won't work. Do you know of a source of convex oval glass?

A. Contact B & L Antiqurie, 6217 South Lake Shore Road, Lexington, MI 48450, for information on custom-cut glass for your picture frames.

Q. I have an old oak high chair that converts to a stroller. It has been handed down through many generations in my family. I have a problem, however, in that it has no tray. A friend of mine felt you could help me locate a source from which I could obtain one. I am expecting our first child in three months and would like very much to be able to use this high chair.

A. That would be quite fitting, especially considering the fact that the chair has been in the family for so long.

Write to Old Hotel Antiques, P.O. Box 94, Sutter Creek, CA 95685, for information on their reproduction high-chair trays. Your other option would be having a woodworker make one specifically for your high chair, using another old one for a model. If none of the antique shops in your area have similar high chairs from which the design for yours could be copied, I would suggest going to the public library, where you should be able to find a picture or drawing of your chair in one of the antique books. Your type of collapsible high chair was quite popular during the late 1800s and early 1900s and has increased in value drastically in recent years.

Q. At an auction recently my husband and I bought a large icebox—we don't know what else it could be. It is made of poplar, we have been told, and is 30 inches deep, 30 inches wide and 54 inches tall. It opens at the top and bottom and has two separate compartments. The frame portion of the whole cabinet is painted false graining. The midsections of the doors are composed of strips of wood glued together. It has cast-iron hardware that is very ornate. The latches at the top and bottom are different sizes, but the same design. My problem is that one latch catch is broken and the other is a replacement. I'd like to replace both. I'd be happiest with old catches, but would settle for reproductions. Do you know of a company or individual that could help me?

Also, do we really have an icebox? The lining is gone inside both sections but, due to the construction, we feel sure it had one. Also the top compartment has a half-inch round hole that has been plugged. Would this have been a drain hole?

A. It sure would have been and, yes, you most certainly have an icebox—a false grained one at that, which is unusual to say the least.

Unfortunately, finding hardware to match is next to impossible. If you check with some of the hardware companies that advertise in antique magazines and newspapers you can see what styles they have to offer. Naturally these will all be reproductions.

What you might want to do is to check to see if you can have the broken catch repaired, perhaps by a welder, or a duplicate cast. If you don't know of anyone who does casting, several of the hardware companies whose catalogues we just spoke of, Horton Brasses, Box 95, Nooks Hill Road, Cromwell, CT 06416, for instance, offer a casting service. With the demand for and value of iceboxes today, it is certainly worth the extra investment of time and money to keep your hardware intact and original, or as close to original as possible.

Q. I am in need of a round leather chair seat 13 inches in diameter. Can you give me any addresses of suppliers? Thank you.

A. Many of the chair seats you are referring to actually aren't leather, but are a fiberboard, which can be trimmed to size and even stained if you desire. One company that sells both actual leather and fiber seats is The Woodworkers' Store, 21801 Industrial Blvd., Rogers, MN 55374.

Reproduction fiber chair seats are offered in a variety of patterns and are amazingly easy to install. A sharp razor blade is all that is needed to cut the square seat to the necessary shape, and upholstery tacks secure it firmly in place.

Q. I have made my find of a lifetime. I found, at a yard sale of all places, a No. 7 Shaker rocker with the original label intact inside the right-hand rocker. I'm sure it still has the original finish on it and all I plan to do is clean it, but I will have to replace the seat. The cloth tape is completely worn through to where you can't even sit on it. I want to replace it with Shaker cloth tape just like the original, but haven't been able to locate either a source or directions for doing it. Can you help?

A. I think so. Write to Shaker Workshops, P.O. Box 1028, Concord, MA 01742, and ask for their catalogue. For one dollar they will send you ten sample tapes for you to select a color or you can simply send a small piece of the original.

As for directions, they will supply them with your order. And, as for those of you who have given up on yard sales, take heed. The finds are still out there, regardless of whether or not you are.

Tip—The National Trust for Historic Preservation is among the groups feeling the pinch of economic cutbacks. If you are interested in becoming a member, write them at 1785 Massachusetts Avenue NW, Washington, DC 20036. In addition to their fine work, they publish one of the best magazines for antiquers, preservationists and history lovers in the United States. Support and join the Trust.

Q. I have a 1918 Grand Rapids *Press* newspaper with the headline TRUCE. It was the day World War I ended. The paper is in fair condition and still very readable. How could I find out how much this or something like it I might find in the future is worth?

I also have my grandfather's pocket watch. Are there price guides for watches so I could find out how much it is worth?

A. You might like to know about the International Newspaper Collector's Club, P.O. Box 7271, Phoenix, AZ 85011, which has its own publication. They can help point you toward the best price guides for old newspapers.

As for your grandfather's pocket watch, consult Cooksey Shugart's book *The Complete Guide to American Pocket Watches*, published by Overstreet Publications, 780 Hunt Cliff Drive NW, Cleveland, TN 37311.

Q. One problem I keep running into in my restoration work is missing pieces of trim. So far they have either been simple or small enough that I could carve them or even make a rough duplication with my router and then file them to shape.

Right now I have a large china cupboard that is missing a very complex piece of trim along one side. I know I can't make a replacement myself and I hate the thought of taking the trim off the other side just to make it balance. I'm not in a situation where I can go out and invest two hundred dollars in fancy router bits either. Do you have any suggestions or sources for refinishers like myself who really aren't woodworkers?

A. You've made a good point. There's no need for a refinisher to also be a master cabinetmaker, locksmith, mirror resilverer or metalworker. Just as important as being able to do any of these tasks yourself is knowing who can do it even better.

Cabinetmakers find it essential to have a commercial shaper and dozens of bits on hand for the many styles of moldings they produce. Instead of investing in numerous router bits, which, by the way, aren't as clean cutting as a shaper, contact several cabinet shops to see which would be interested in helping you out. You'll find them even more apt to be helpful if you can provide the piece of wood (two or three are even better so they can experiment without ruining your only piece) cut to the correct length, width and thickness. Send the matching piece or a full-scale tracing along as a model. The more you can do to make the job a little easier, the more likely they will be to take on a small job.

Tip—If you find yourself using a good deal of sandpaper, check with one of your local cabinetmakers to see if you can buy it directly from him. You may have to buy fifty sheets at a time, but you stand a good chance of getting it at a little more than half the retail price.

Q. I am trying to refinish an old trunk, but I have not been able to decide how to remove the fabric that is between the slats across the top and around the sides. I want to get it down to bare wood so I can sand and refinish it like another trunk I saw.

Also, I have not been able to obtain a hinge to keep the trunk open or the leather side handles. Where can one get a book on refinishing trunks? I had one years ago but misplaced it.

A. There are two or three companies advertising in the backs of hobby, antique and crafts magazines that sell parts for the many different styles of trunks that have survived over the years. Two that I have seen are Charlotte Ford Trunks, Box 536, Spearman, TX 79081; and Gerry Sharp, Trunk Doctor, 8495 Culebra Road, San Antonio, TX 78251. Both offer catalogues and books, as does the Antique Trunk Company, 3706 West 169th Street, Cleveland, OH 44111.

As for getting the fabric off the sides of your trunk, try laying a damp cloth across it for a short period of time. The old glues were usually water soluable and should dissolve readily. Be careful not to let the water remain on the trunk too long, however, or it may warp the wood underneath.

Q. Where can I order veneer?

A. Artistry in Veneers, Inc., 450 Oaktree Avenue, South Plainfield, NJ 07080; and Bob Morgan Woodworking Supplies, 1123 Bardstown Road, Louisville, KY 40204. These are only two of several companies that sell veneer. Check the classified section of crafts, woodworking and antique publications for others.

Q. I repair old furniture as a hobby and for some extra income, and it seems like I get a lot of tables and desks that have cigarette burns along the edges. On the ones made from solid wood I fill and sand, but on veneer pieces I end up spending all my time trying to get a veneer patch to fit in.

I heard of a tool called a veneer punch that is supposed to help on these jobs. Do you know where I could order one?

A. A veneer punch is handy if you do a lot of veneer patching, but somewhat expensive. It is a stamping tool approximately ¾ inch in diameter, but instead of being perfectly round, it has an irregular shape.

You take the punch and tap it over the burned area, remove the old veneer, then repeat over your new veneer. The two cutouts will then be identical in shape, and the new patch will slip in like the last piece in a puzzle.

You can order a veneer punch from Constantine's, 2050 Eastchester Road, Bronx, NY 10461, or you might see if a local toolmaker will make you one in trade for some refinishing.

Even though it means re-moving more wood, try to make your veneer patch lines run in the direction of the grain. Square or rect-angular patches are more obvious than triangles or di-amond shapes, so it becomes a situation where more cut-ting is better than less. Re-gardless of the shape or size of the patch, however, the closer the match of the pat-tern of the grain the better it will blend in.

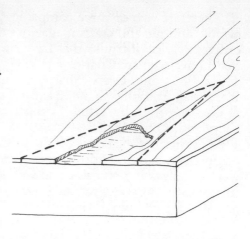

Q. I need some help locating some brass feet for Duncan Phyfe furniture. I have three tables, all with different size feet and have the opportunity to buy this type furniture in various auctions; I will pass it by many times, however, because of my inability to find replacement pieces.

A. Write to The Woodworkers' Store, 21801 Industrial Blvd., Rogers, MN 55374, for their catalogue, which lists three dif-ferent sizes of eagle claw feet for Duncan Phyfe tables.

Q. I have an old oak bed that I'm trying to find hardware for so I can complete it with side rails. I need all new hardware, but it has to be a special kind to fit the carved opening in the headboard and foot and in the rails as well. I have part of the original set that was made out of cast iron, but need to know where I can order a complete new set.

A. I know the type of cast-iron bed hardware you are talking about; it was common on beds made around and before the Civil War. The cast-iron sleeve fits into the post, and the cast piece that fits into each end of the rail looks like a horseshoe with two notched protrusions.

Unfortunately I haven't found a company that reproduces this type of hardware, primarily because there is so much variation from one bed to another. You will need to send your existing pieces to someone who casts reproductions and have him or her make you a complete set. Several of the major companies that make hardware also cast specialty pieces, so check with them.

Q. I have recently purchased a wicker rocker that has some very rotten wicker in it, but it could be restored if I could find the wicker. All I can find is reed basket material. Could you please put me in touch with a source for wicker?

A. Write to these companies for their catalogues: Connecticut Cane and Reed Co., P.O. Box 1276, Manchester, CT 06040; H. H. Perkins Co., 10 South Bradley Road, Woodbridge, CT 06525; Cane and Basket Supply Co., 1283 South Cochran Avenue, Los Angeles, CA 90019.

Q. We are in the midst of restoring a turn-of-the-century house and have been looking in several antique shops for the fancy "gingerbread" decorative wood pieces that were used in doorways and in corners of these old houses. We've figured out that it will take years for us to find all original pieces and so are now looking for someplace that reproduces them. Do you happen to know of any company that does?

A. Vintage Wood Works, 37 Main Street, Quinlan, TX 75474, advertises a variety of decorative fretwork, including running trim, gingerbread, brackets and ball-and-dowel fans. They ask for one dollar in return for their catalogue.

Q. Over the weekend at a garage sale only a couple of blocks from where I live, I got a great deal on a pair of stacking oak bookcases. I got the base, two sections and a top all for only twenty dollars. I checked with some of the antique shops and when I saw how much they wanted for them I nearly died.

One reason the bookcases were so cheap is because they don't have the glass sliding doors anymore. I didn't care because I figured, at that price, I could buy some to put on them. Is there someplace that makes new doors for them?

A. I'm not aware of any company that mass-produces new doors for stacking oak bookcases. With the large variety of sizes that were manufactured, I doubt if it would be a profitable venture.

I would recommend that you check with several of your local refinishers and dealers, especially the ones who buy antiques in the rough, to see if any of them have spare parts lying around. If not, attempt to borrow a door that comes very close to fitting and take it and your two bookcase sections to several cabinet shops or woodworkers for estimates on having two doors custom made.

As you said yourself, at that price you can afford to have them made.

Tip—Solid brass knobs for stacking oak bookcases are being reproduced by Heirloom Brass Co., Box 146, Dundas, MN 55019. Send a large, self-addressed, stamped manila envelope for a copy of their catalogue.

Q. Can you give us a source for a lock for a rolltop desk? We bought an old oak rolltop from a dealer, and someone had taken the lock out. We are in the process of restoring it and want to make it complete.

A. Write to the Wise Company, P.O. Box 118, Arabi, LA 70032. They stock a variety of locks and catches for rolltops, cabinet doors and chests and also offer hard-to-find hinges, escutcheons, wooden parts and other hardware.

Q. Can you direct me to a source of either legitimate old porcelain castors or new reproductions? We have a five-legged walnut drop-leaf table needing castors, and I saw a similar table in an antique shop with porcelain rather than the wooden castors. I haven't been able to find any in our local hardware stores, and no one I've talked to seems to think they are still available.

A. The best but certainly not the most reliable sources of old porcelain castors are restoration shops, antique dealers, secondhand furniture stores and flea markets. Most of these, however, either will not have complete sets or will not readily part with them. Reproductions can be ordered through the catalogue of The Woodworkers' Store, 21801 Industrial Blvd., Rogers, MN 55374.

Q. I have a number of older lamps, both floor and table models. The old shades I have for them are in sad shape and new shades

I've seen just don't look right. Do you know of any places around the country that sell reproductions of old-style fabric-type lamp shades?

A. Sure do, lots of them. We don't have enough room to list them all, but here are a few to start with: Schutte's Lamp Supply, 503 West Spring Street, Lima, OH 45801; Shades Of The Past, 166 Allied Street, Manchester, NH 03103; and Van Parys Studio, 6338 Germantown Avenue, Philadelphia, PA 19144.

Q. Some years ago I recaned some antique chairs. I used plastic cane instead of natural and found that it was much easier to use. Now I have some more chairs to cane, but cannot find anyone who carries plastic cane.

Can you give me the address of a company where I can order it?

A. There are at least two companies that I know of that handle plastic cane in addition to natural. They are H. H. Perkins Co., 10 South Bradley Road, Woodbridge, CT 06525; and Cane and Basket Supply Co., 1283 Cochran Avenue, Los Angeles, CA 90019. Both companies have catalogues that they will send you upon request.

I cannot resist one quick comment, however, before you send for your plastic cane. Both natural and plastic cane seem to have about the same life expectancy and both seem to have about the same resistance to spills, stains and other lurking evils. Plastic cane is easier to work with, but most antique dealers will tell you that chairs with plastic cane do not have the same antique appeal as those with natural cane in them.

I have worked with both and, though the plastic was faster to weave, I found the natural cane to be more appropriate for antiques. Naturally, the choice is yours, but in addition to momentary convenience, consider the long-term effect.

Q. I have a very plain oak commode that I refinished several years ago after buying it at an auction. I have always been bothered by the fact that the splashboard across the back is missing, leaving me with a commode top with a gap across the back. I am going to take a woodworking class through our local community college next month, and I want to make a splashboard for my commode, but don't know exactly what it should look like. I have a general idea of splashboards and their approximate sizes, but how do I design one that will look right on my commode?

A. I would suggest two sources, one primary and the other secondary. The best place to start is with your commode. From it you can determine the exact length and the thickness of the splashboard.

The design of the splashboard should be as closely matched to the design of the commode as possible. Study the design of the board at the bottom of the commode under the bottom drawer and door. Check as well the bottoms of the side panels. If they have a curved design or a special cutout, attempt to duplicate that in your splashboard. If they are plain and simple, so should your splashboard be.

To get an idea of the height of your splashboard, take the dimensions of your commode with you to several antique shops and compare them to the commodes you find there. Your splashboard should be similar in size to those on commodes like yours. If you want to see several different splashboard designs, spend an hour of research in the antique section of your library.

Q. I'm trying to find disposable syringes to use to inject glue into fine cracks. I've been told drugstores can't sell them because they think you're going to use them for drugs. I don't like the metal ones for sale in woodworking catalogues because they clog up and are impossible to clean. Do you have a source or at least some suggestions?

A. Possibly. See your family doctor or veterinarian and tell him or her what you want them for. If they know you well enough and appreciate antiques, you should be able to get your syringes without any trouble. Also, and this just came in a short while ago, I was told that farm-supply stores carry them as well, so you shouldn't be without glue syringes for long.

Q. I have a 54-inch round oak table with four leaves. My problem is that when I put the leaves in they don't match up perfectly. At some points one edge is higher or lower than the leaf next to it. This makes the table difficult to use, as glasses get tipped over and plates won't sit level. Is there anything I can get to correct this?

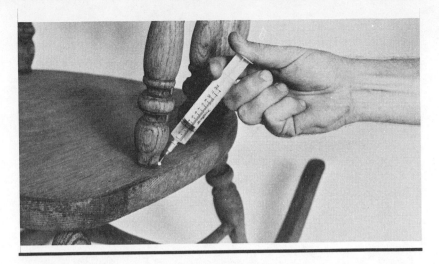

A. Several woodworking companies offer a 2-inch tabletop leveler, also called an evener. The narrow evener is attached to the underside of the table or leaf at the high point with one or two

small screws. When the leaves are pushed together, the lower board slides onto the protruding evener and next to the other leaf. The eveners cost less than ten cents each and can be installed in a matter of minutes. They make for a cheap and easy solution to a frustrating problem.

11 / Keeping Them in Shape

I've always believed that if you can't use an antique, if you can't sit on it, eat off it, rock in it, write on it, use it as it was meant to be used, then why have it? If it's too good to use or too fragile, give it to someone else in the family or donate it to a museum or your local historical society; take the tax deduction and get an antique you can actually put to use.

What that means, then, is that you are going to have to do some occasional maintenance on your antiques. Dusting, waxing, checking veneer, testing glue joints and watching for infestation are a few of the more common tasks you'll need to get in the habit of doing, but the few minutes they take are but a small price to pay for safe, sturdy antiques, and nothing compared to the cost of having a good piece repaired or restored. Read on and learn—and save:

Q. Which is better to use on my furniture and antiques, lemon oil or paste wax?

Paste wax or lemon oil? Both have their uses; you just have to decide which you need for each of your antiques. Keep both on hand—and use them.

A. Both have their strong and weak points—and both have their proponents and opponents—so regardless of what you hear, realize that both have their place on your shelf of household products.

Lemon oil is preferred by many antique dealers, collectors and refinishers for two main reasons: first, it is easy to use and, second, it doesn't leave a sticky film on the finish. It also doesn't give the finish any protection, so it should only be used over a good existing finish. Lemon oil's primary function is to help your cloth pick up dust; if the wood has been scratched, lemon oil will seal the pores and offer some temporary protection, but that is not its job.

To use it properly, shake a few drops onto your rag or directly onto the surface of the wood and wipe the dust off, rubbing only in the direction of the grain. Make sure your rag is adequately moistened with the lemon oil; if not, the combination of the dust and your dry rag will act as fine sandpaper and can actually leave scratches in your finish. Using too much lemon oil won't hurt anything, but since it isn't absorbed by the finish, doesn't do any good. Wipe with the grain, folding your cloth over as it becomes soiled. As soon as you have finished, switch to a clean, dry soft cloth to buff the wood. This will absorb any remaining lemon oil and will leave your antique with a nice satin sheen.

Paste wax is designed to give both the wood and the finish an additional layer of protection. As you might expect, then, it is more difficult to apply than lemon oil; the other problem is that paste wax can appear streaky and will, in fact, attract dirt. Once a year it will need to be scrubbed off with mineral spirits and a new coat rubbed in. In the meantime, however, it will help protect the wood and the finish from moisture and abuse.

Experience has shown, then, that on newly refinished pieces or those with plenty of good finish, lemon oil is preferred for dusting and polishing. On pieces that either have a weak finish or are in need of all the protection they can get, paste wax is worth the extra effort.

Q. I just came from a Questors meeting at which one of the members related a conversation she had with a professional refinisher. It seems that he claims lemon oil, wax and all commercial polishes (he mentioned several by name but I'd better not) are harmful to furniture finishes and will eventually destroy them.

I was skeptical at first, but I don't want to dismiss it if there's a possibility he could be right. I have been using lemon oil on all my antiques for years and I would hate to think that I have been slowly destroying the finishes. I should mention that this refinisher recommended that the woman use only soap and water to clean all her furniture and no oils, waxes or polishes whatsoever. I thought water could be more harmful myself, but wanted your opinion.

A. I'm walking on thin ice when I comment on a second- or thirdhand conversation, but I will say that I have never heard of lemon oil or wax being harmful to a good finish. Several household cleaners will damage a finish, but no one in their right mind would spray or pour the same thing they use to clean their sink on their antiques, would they?

What probably ignited the conversation was the use of commercial aerosol polishes. Television advertisers have bombarded us with propaganda and promises regarding their products, perhaps to counteract the belief that some of the ingredients of the aerosol sprays will eventually damage wood finishes.

As for the soap and water treatment, certainly, if not used in excess, it would clean a good finish without harming the wood, but it won't give it a shine nor will it offer any protection for the finish. Until shown a reason to change, I will continue to recommend using lemon oil for dusting and polishing an existing finish and applying paste wax on surfaces that will receive excessive use, such as table and dresser tops.

Q. What is the proper way to apply paste wax? I just waxed my round oak table and it looks streaky. It looked fine before I waxed it, so I know the problem wasn't in the wood or the varnish.

A. Paste wax is only as clear as the finish under it, so you first have to start with a perfectly clean surface. Wash the finish with a rag dipped in mineral spirits, follow by wiping with a soft, absorbant cloth, then give it time to dry.

To properly apply paste wax, dip a clean piece of cheesecloth in a can of high-quality paste wax and apply a thin coat to a small area—and here is where I differ from the usual directions—rubbing *with* the grain and *not* in a tight circular motion. That way if the wax does dry before you get it completely buffed, the application marks will be less evident than if they were in circles. The directions may also recommend waiting fifteen minutes before buffing, but if you do you'll find the wax so hard that you'll always see streaks and application strokes.

Since you put on a thin coat, three to five minutes should be long enough to wait before buffing. You don't want to leave anything but a thin, hard layer of wax, so switch to a clean piece of cheesecloth and buff with the grain to erase your application marks. To minimize streaks, keep folding your cloth as it fills up with wax. You may feel as if you're taking all of the wax off, but you're not. What you will leave is a thin, hard layer of wax that will, without distorting the finish, protect it from normal abuse.

Tip—If you like the added protection of a coat of paste wax on your tabletops, wait at least a week for your new varnish to cure before applying it. Even though your varnish may feel dry only hours after you brushed it on, it needs the additional time to finish hardening before you seal it with the wax.

Q. With winter due again here in the Midwest, what suggestions would you make regarding safeguarding our antiques and wooden furniture against the drastic drop in humidity we are going to experience? Every winter it seems chairs that were fine just a few weeks before become wobbly, and I'm worried about tabletops, dresser sides and drawers drying out and splitting.

A. You have already taken the first step in preventing damage to your antiques and that is just being aware of the problem. Dry air presents a real danger to both old woods and the animal glues used to hold them together, but, unless we realize that, we may be subjecting our antiques to a slow death.

Obviously the most desirable solution would be to hold the humidity in the air at a constant and comfortable level. Once it drops below 35 to 40 percent, antiques are susceptible to damage from what would otherwise be considered normal stress. Humidifiers, either central, room or improvised, offer a good deal of help in protecting antiques against the evils of dry air. With or without them, however, there are precautions you can take. Vulnerable pieces should be moved away from direct sources of heat, such as fireplaces, heating stoves, furnace vents and air registers. If this is impossible, install deflectors to keep the dry air from blowing directly on the wood.

Antiques that have been properly refinished or that still have a good finish won't suffer a good deal of damage under normal circumstances, but all pieces should be checked to make sure the undersides have a protective coating as well. If the bottoms of your tables and chairs and the insides of your dressers never had a finish or if the pieces were stripped but refinished only on the outsides, you had best seal the pores to prevent your furniture from drying out and splitting.

Sealers can range from a mixture of three parts denatured alcohol and one part shellac, to commercial sanding sealers, to some old varnish you have saved but don't want to trust on a good project, to any type of oil finish. Turn your pieces upside down on an old blanket and coat all parts using whichever sealer you prefer. Be careful, however, that you don't run your sealer down the sides or through cracks onto your good finish.

Finally, check your antiques regularly. If you aren't sure if a suspicious crack is old or new, mark it with a piece of chalk and check its progress. If it spreads, immediate attention must be paid, or come spring it will be the refinisher you'll be paying.

．．．

How about a number of tips from our readers:

Tip—This is a good time to check all your antique wooden kitchen utensils (butter molds, paddles, pounders, etc.) for signs of drying out and splitting. Clean with a damp sponge, let dry and coat with vegetable oil. Wipe oil off thirty minutes later, after the wood has absorbed all it can.

Tip—As the seasons change and the sun's arc travels up and down the sky, we need to make sure none of our antiques are being exposed to long periods of direct sunlight. If precautions aren't taken, such as pulling drapes or moving furniture, excessive bleaching can result, along with permanent damage to the finish. Besides, we all like an excuse to rearrange the furniture anyway.

Tip—Check the edges of any veneered drawers, table skirts, and dresser tops on a regular basis. If the veneer has come loose, simply squirt some glue under it and weight down overnight. Once those loose pieces break off, they get lost and you end up with a patch instead of a perfect antique.

Tip—Check flowerpots, lamps, statues, ashtrays, and any other knickknacks on your tables, dressers and desks regularly to make sure no water has leaked, none of the felt pads have come off and no damage is being done to your antiques. As trite as it may seem, an ounce of prevention is definitely worth a pound of cure in the antique restoration business.

．．．

But if you are too late:

Tip—Surface scratches caused by bowls, picture frames or other items commonly found on coffee tables, buffets and the like can often be removed by rubbing gently with #0000 steel wool moistened with lemon oil or a commercial scratch remover.

Wicker furniture was at the zenith of its popularity during the final years of the reign of Queen Victoria, but then until a few years ago it suffered the disgrace of being relegated to attics, basements, garages, barns and dumps. That which was used was too often painted, but now wicker is enjoying a return to favor, with complete sets still in their natural state commanding rising prices. Like all antiques, however, wicker needs attention periodically:

Q. I have a set of wicker furniture that we leave outside on our sun porch during the summer, but bring indoors during the winter. The set consists of two matching chairs, one of which is a rocker, a side table and a love seat.

74410½ Lady's Fancy Reed Rocker, a perfect little beauty. Lots of fine work and very showy. Very strong and comfortable. Weight, 11 pounds. Price, natural reed........$4.00
New shellac finish....   4.90
74411 Man's Large Arm Rocker, same as 74410½, except much larger. Very showy and durable. Weight, about 15 pounds. Natural reed, only........$5.77
New shellac finish........ 6.65

74410½

74412 Lady's Rocker, made of very fine reed, with a full solid roll. Exceedingly strong and has high back. An ornament to any home. Weight, 12 pounds. Natural reed...$4.25
New shellac finish.. ... 5.1C
74413 Gentleman's Large Arm Rocker of the same pattern as 74412 High back; very strong aud very comfortable, strong enough for any man. Weight. 16 pounds. Natural reed.$6.00
New shellac finish....... 6.90

74414 A Lady's Full Roll Comfort Rocker, solid roll all around the rocker, with a reed seat. These comfort rockers are the most complete and most durable of any rocker made. Has a good high arm and medium high back. Weight, 12 pounds. Never sold less than $6.00.
Our price, natural reel.$4.45
New shellac finish..... 5.35
74415 Gentleman's Large Arm Rocker, same style and pattern as 74414; high back and very comfortable; a household comfort. Never
74414 sold for zess than $8 00. Weight, 15 pounds.
Our price, natural reed......................$5.75
New shellac finish................................ 6.65

An ad appearing in the 1895 edition of the Montgomery Ward catalogue, which offered over two dozen different styles and varieties of wicker rocking chairs alone.

Our problem—really our concern—is that the wicker may be deteriorating. It is completely natural and seems to be drying out in many places. My husband says we should paint it to keep it from rotting away, but I'm not so sure. Is there another way we can preserve the wicker without painting it?

A. Sure is, so don't even consider painting it.

As strange as it may seem, take your wicker furniture out into the yard or driveway and give it a bath—actually, a shower. If you've got a hose give the wicker a light misting, otherwise use a bucket and a rag to wet each piece. The wicker needs to have some of the moisture it has lost replaced, so give it a bath and then let it sit for a day in the shade to revive.

The following day prepare a mixture of one part varnish and two parts mineral spirits and brush it on liberally over the entire piece. Let the furniture sit for another day to finish drying and then it should be ready for another year's use.

• • •

Along with wicker come questions on caning, which was popular at the same time, went through a period of neglect and now is widely sought after, especially in pressed-back chairs and rockers. The most often asked question concerns protecting cane against everything from food to feet:

Q. I have just finished my first caning project and need to know if I should put a coat of finish over the cane to protect it.

A. No. Modern cane comes with the top side sealed and the bottom left open to breathe. Additional finish on either side will only make the cane more brittle and will eventually shorten its life span. You can clean cane with a damp sponge and, if it begins to lose its tension, turn the chair over and lay a wet towel over the bottom side of the cane for three or four hours. The cane should tighten when it dries.

Tip—Check the undersides of your cane seats to make sure the wood around the opening in the chair isn't beginning to crack. Many times the tension of the cane will actually pull the wood apart. If this is happening, inject glue in the crack and put in a couple of screws to give the wood extra support (see illustration on facing page).

Sagging cane seats can be partially revived by placing a wet towel across the underside of the cane overnight and then letting it dry the next day. As the moisture evaporates, the strands will tighten and much of the slack will disappear.

It is not unusual for cracks to develop between the holes in cane-seat chairs after eighty years or so of use. The pressure exerted by the stretched cane is enough to literally pull the wood apart.

Dry wicker and cane can occasionally pose problems, but they're nothing compared to an infestation of powder-post beetles. They are the little guys that make the wormholes that people like to see in their furniture because it makes them think it's really old. When I see them I get scared, because I know what they can do to a piece of wood—and a valuable old antique.

Q. I have two very important emergency questions. First, is there any foolproof way to detect active worm infestation in wooden furniture? I have a beautiful flatwall cupboard that has a series of small holes concentrated on one drawer front, but also in a number of other places on the piece.

Second, is there any way to cure worm infestation? A delicate library table that has been next to the cupboard for quite a long time also has one of these holes and it is not in an area where you would expect to find a nail.

A. The only foolproof way I know of to detect active powder-post beetles is to cut the piece in half and look for them. Since that's not too bright an idea, we'll have to drop back to a couple of less dependable methods.

First, count the number of holes. I have an old oak bed in which once a week for the past seven years I have counted the same seven wormholes. Until there's eight, I'll sleep at night. Second, clean out the holes and then watch for any accumulation of wood dust at the entrance. New dust is a bad sign; if you've got wood dust you've got trouble. Government regulations have placed many of the toxic chemicals formerly used to control powder-post beetles solely in the hands of certified pest exterminators, so check with one of them or with someone in the lawn and garden field for help if you need it.

As for your delicate library table, I have never heard of powder-post beetles moving from one piece of furniture to another unless they were in direct contact (and by direct I mean one sitting atop the other) for a long, long time. My guess is your wormhole is a nail hole—even if it isn't where you would expect a nail to be. (The truth is anyone who picks up a hammer and nail immediately loses all good judgment.) Get a magnifying glass and study the hole closely; a wormhole will be irregular in shape while a nail hole should be nearly perfectly round.

One other reader offers this suggestion for dealing with powder-post beetles once they are discovered:

Q. I had certified pest exterminators in to examine holes that turned out to have been made by powder-post beetles. The holes are in wood in my basement. The exterminator said the beetles will systematically work their way through all wood, so it is important to eliminate them before they get upstairs into the furniture, where treatment is difficult without harming the pieces.

The exterminator said to apply lindane with a pump-spray. He said the spray application should be made everywhere—inside, outside, behind, underneath. He pointed out that the application will kill the pests as they work their way in and out of the wood.

A. Thank you for your letter and the valuable information. Another reader took it a step further and, using a syringe, injected a lindane solution into the wormholes in her furniture. At last report the powder-post beetles had not spread, so perhaps this is the best we can do to repel them without harming our antiques.

Tip—One of our regular readers also responded to an earlier column and sent us this suggestion: "As an antique dealer, through the years I have successfully treated powder-post beetles with wood preservatives containing copper. The tarnish-green colored liquid may be brushed liberally on bare wood or over any finish, which it will not harm. The last brand name I used was Coppo, but there are others. Hope this helps."

. . .

Tips, tips and more tips:

Tip—Do not use common household oil to lubricate clockworks, for it will attract dust, which will eventually jam the gears. Keep a small can of clock oil (available at any clock repair shop) just for your old clocks.

Tip—If the doors on your antique bookcase, desk or buffet sag or stick, check to see if the entire piece is sitting level. If the front is lower than the back, the doors won't open or close properly—and all you need to do is insert a thin piece of wood under the lower legs.

Tip—Personal experience has taught me that describing and identifying stolen antiques can be difficult and frustrating. Before it happens to you, inscribe identification numbers in obscure spots on your good antiques and tuck the list away with your important papers. It could get your stolen property back some day.

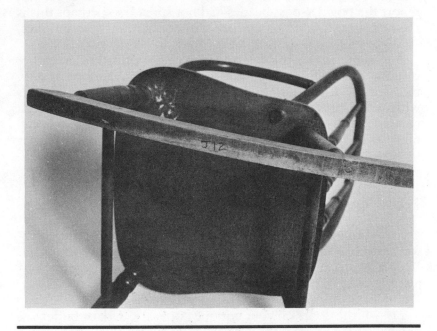

Inscribe identification numbers in inconspicuous places on your antiques and keep the list with your important papers.